2

THE DISTRIBUTION OF INCOMES IN THE UNITED STATES

STUDIES IN HISTORY, ECONOMICS AND PUBLIC LAW

EDITED BY THE FACULTY OF POLITICAL SCIENCE
OF COLUMBIA UNIVERSITY

Volume LII]   [Number 2
Whole Number 129

THE DISTRIBUTION OF INCOMES
IN THE UNITED STATES

BY

FRANK HATCH STREIGHTOFF

AMS PRESS
NEW YORK

98081

COLUMBIA UNIVERSITY
STUDIES IN THE
SOCIAL SCIENCES

129

The Series was formerly known as *Studies in History,
Economics and Public Law.*

Reprinted with the permission of Columbia University Press
From the edition of 1912, New York
First AMS EDITION published 1968
Manufactured in the United States of America

Library of Congress Catalogue Card Number: 68-56688

AMS PRESS, INC.
New York, N.Y. 10003

PREFACE

To Professors Edwin R. A. Seligman, Henry R. Seager, Henry L. Moore, and Robert E. Chaddock, the writer is indebted for much help in the preparation of this monograph. Especially is he grateful to Professor Seager for advice, criticism, and encouragement.

CONTENTS

CHAPTER IV

The Sources of American Income Statistics

CHAPTER V

Previous Treatment of American Income Statistics

CHAPTER VI

Statistics of the Distribution of Wages

LIST OF TABLES

CHAPTER I

THE UTILITY OF INCOME STATISTICS

IN the evolution of certain industries, " costing " and the standardization of efficiency are potent factors. As, in the proper conduct of a large business, it is necessary to have within easy reach all the facts which would bear upon the solution of any great problem that may arise, so the possibility of perfect legislation is doubtful unless the law-makers possess an intimate knowledge of the conditions with which they are attempting to cope. This principle is recognized practically in the habit of appointing commissions to investigate important state and national questions. There is a considerable group of problems which must be considered, both by these legislative committees and by individuals, largely with reference to the distribution of incomes. For instance, the present organization of industry is accompanied by certain demands for social insurance—old-age pensions, workmen's compensation, sick benefits, and unemployment relief. Only by one who is well acquainted with the resources of the family groups in the classes involved can the desirability, or the necessity, of adopting any one of these proposals, or any combination of them, be discussed intelligently. The advisability of old-age pensions, for example, depends largely upon the answers of two questions: (1) Do a large majority of American workingmen have the opportunity, supposing they are no more thriftless than lack of education and their environment inevitably make them, to provide for their own years of decline? and (2) Can the large majority of Americans, if necessary, support aged parents without real injury to themselves and their families, and how often does the necessity arise? These two questions cannot be answered without statistics of the distribution of incomes. But even if the legislators have decided to introduce a system of old-age pensions, they must determine the method of financing the new institutions; and here ability to make compulsory contributions to the fund, or to pay taxes, should be considered in the light of incomes.

Again, if the proposed Sixteenth Amendment is passed, and if an income tax is to be imposed, would it not be wise in fixing rates to consider the probable yield? Can this be done without knowledge of the base of the tax? And if this base is personal income, as it was in the impost of Civil War times, statistics of income are needed. Similar considerations should be recognized in imposing other taxes.

Minimum wage laws and child-labor regulations can hardly be classed either with social insurance in the narrower sense or with the income tax, and yet they are measures of such deep economic significance that they demand of the legislature scientific consideration as well as political attention—a deep knowledge of the actual state of affairs and of the probable effects of new enactments. Finally, it is hardly a matter of doubt that the majority of influential Americans are in ignorance of the actual amount and diffusion of well-being in their own country. Conclusive statistics are necessary to show them the facts, really to acquaint the citizens with one another. The attitude of many people upon the great social questions of the day is to a large extent influenced by their conception of the present distribution of well-being, and of the tendency toward improvement or the reverse.

So, in the framing of social legislation, in the assessing of certain kinds of taxes, and in influencing individual and public opinion, statistics of the distribution of incomes have a real utility.

It is the purpose of this essay to show that at present the United States lacks the income statistics that might have this utility, to point out what the figures, which are available, seem to indicate, and to suggest a plan by which more satisfactory statistics of incomes may be secured.

CHAPTER II

Ideal Income Statistics

THE exact character of the ideal compilation of income statistics depends on the purpose in view. If, for example, following the lead of Professor Henry L. Moore, it is determined to submit to empirical test the current wage theories, the minimum necessary information concerning each individual would doubtless include, besides his actual earnings: (1) his race, sex, age, and experience; (2) the industry and exact occupation in which he is employed, the amount of skill involved being expressed, if possible, numerically; (3) the degree of organization of labor in the occupation, the membership or non-membership of the individual in the union, and the character of the employing establishment; (4) the size of the plant in which he is employed, the amount of capital invested, and the value of machinery and of net output, per laborer, in the whole business and in the department; (5) his geographical location, and the regularity of employment in his trade. These data should be supplemented by other studies of the standards and costs of living, and of the purchasing power of money; the presentation would involve an indefinite number of two and three dimension tables. The first comprehensive attempt to furnish such a study for the United States has been made by the Bureau of Labor in its elaborate *Report on Condition of Woman and Child Wage-Earners in the United States*, a work which contains much that may be turned to account

18   [190

by the theorist. For the objects mentioned in the preceding
chapter, however, no such elaboration is necessary; in truth,
it might conceal the vital concerns under a mass of detail.
The following sketch will, therefore, be confined to a description
of the statistics necessary for an intelligent grasp
of those great social questions which are now rising to
recognized importance.

To be really complete, these income statistics must include
returns from every gainfully-employed person,
whether a high-salaried corporation official, or a child in
the tenement. In addition, pensioners and individuals living
upon the earnings of property should be tabulated, and
the final summary should be a classification of the entire
number of income-receiving individuals and families by the
size of their total incomes. Doubtless any attempt to investigate
the earnings of " business " men would to-day be
deemed " inquisitorial " and be stoutly resisted; but the impossibility
of such a study detracts nothing from its desirability.
The wage earners, however, are those whose interests
are most in need of protection in the crises of life; so,
if it is impossible to secure returns from the men who are
eminently qualified to take care of themselves, the social
reformer may find a sufficient working basis in data covering
the other classes in industrial society.

In the collection of statistics of income, recourse may be
had to three sources; a canvass may seek returns from individuals,
or the data may be gathered through the employers,
or through the officials of labor organizations. The basis
of the figures of earnings and of unemployment compiled
by the New York State Department of Labor is the report
of the secretary of the union; but even with complete returns
from all the " Locals " in the country, a very small
proportion of the gainfully employed would be represented,
since the unskilled, unorganized, numerous but low paid,

workers would be omitted.[1] It would, therefore, be unwise
to build largely upon statistics drawn merely from the organizations of laborers, even if complete confidence could
be placed in the accuracy and extent of the knowledge of
their officials. Of the other two sources of information,
each has its peculiar merits and defects.

An excellent statement of the case in favor of securing
data from employers is the following by Professor Davis R.
Dewey :

In the collection of data it was decided to rely upon the pay-
rolls of employers; only in this way is it possible to secure
returns from all the constituent elements in a given establishment, for it is manifestly impracticable to visit each separate
employee to obtain a personal return ; and, moreover, it is clear
that the pay-roll of the employer states in the most precise
form available the actual rate of pay of each employee. This
method removes all opportunity for either exaggeration or
under-estimation, and also the possibility of substituting a customary wage for the actual one.[2]

This is true; yet in considering the value of the method it
must be recognized that the employer may not be willing
to furnish his pay rolls, that the agent may be careless as
some census takers certainly have been, or that the records
may be confused. To ask the employer to assume the ex-
pense and trouble of filling out the blanks himself, seems
to invite hasty, slip-shod work; nevertheless, where this is
done annually, as in Massachusetts and New Jersey, there
may be established a high standard of accuracy. The one
permanent fault of the pay roll as a source of income statis-

---

[1] There were in 1910 about 2,625,000 members of American trade
unions, United States and Canada, as compared with about 35,000,000
gainfully employed persons in the United States alone. *Bulletin, New
York Department of Labor*, no. 48, Sept. 1911, p. 418.

[2] *Twelfth Census, Report on Employees and Wages*, p. xvi.

tics is the difficulty of deriving annual earnings from weekly or fortnightly records; especially is this true of factory people, who have a habit, in some towns, of shifting frequently from one mill to another, apparently for the sake of variety. Combine this difficulty with the complications which would follow upon the attempt to trace one man through twenty-six or fifty-two separate pay rolls, a man who may have lost some time; then multiply by the number of employees in a large establishment, and the stupendousness of the task of arriving at annual earnings from the records of employers will be clear. Even supposing a satisfactory knowledge of annual earnings, the matter of family incomes is still untouched. The way out, however, is not far to seek; a large number of names may be chosen at random from the pay rolls, and the individuals visited. These individuals may be asked for details as to annual earnings, unemployment, and family incomes. This method has been used by the Bureau of Labor in recent investigations with gratifying results.[1]

An attempt to obtain income statistics by a canvass of individual families would have the advantage of going directly to those who *should* be able to say how much they have earned as individuals during the year, and what the combined family income, including that from property has been. On the other hand, there seem to be many households that would find it impossible to impart even this information, and, barring this complication, if a random selection were made, some industries and occupations might be inadequately represented. In view of all these considerations, the correct conclusion seems to be that the best source for income statistics is the pay roll of the employer, supplemented

[1] See for example the report on *Women in Department Stores,* vol. v of the *Report on Condition of Woman and Child Wage-Earners in the United States,* p. 12 *et seq.*

by individual inquiries among his workers. If it could be made successfuly, however, there is no doubt that a house-to-house canvass would give exactly the data needed for social purposes.

It is by no means imperative that such investigations cover every gainfully-employed individual in the United States, or every family.

In any given locality there is a strong tendency toward uniformity of wages in the same occupation; if, therefore, the occupations are carefully designated, the number of returns for a given occupation need not necessarily be inclusive of all employees engaged in the same kind of work. The more precisely the occupation is described, with regard to sex, age, and gradations of skill, the fewer are the numbers needed.[1]

In determining the size of the sample, each occupation would probably need separate consideration. Of course, the larger the sample, the greater is the probability that the results are truly representative; but it must be borne in mind that for practical purposes it makes very little difference whether the percentage of adult male factory employees earning under $12 per week in 1904 was 62.1 or 62.7; the point that is important is that it was about sixty, and not fifty or seventy. If, on the other hand, the inquiry be directed to ascertaining whether wages are rising or falling, then the fact that from 1890 to 1900 the average rate of weekly pay of male factory hands as shown by the *Dewey Report,* fell from $11.57 to $11.52 is extremely significant. So if absolute accuracy may not be necessary for the consideration of certain great social problems, whenever a question of tendency is involved, it is highly desirable.

Important as are these matters of scope and source in determining the value of income statistics, the manner of

---

[1] *Twelfth Census, Report on Employees, and Wages,* p. xvi, par. 2.

presentation is just as vital to their utility. Arithmetic averages, so easily understood, are probably necessary for comparisons in time and in space; and the application of methods of correlation may disclose new and important uses for this summary expression. The mode, too, if only approximated by inspection, is a more concrete concept than the mean, and thus may show what a normal man might expect to earn in a given occupation at a certain place. But both the average and the mode lose much of their significance if applied to an entire state, or even to one branch of industry. These summary expressions must, therefore, be supplemented by classifications. Weekly wages should be presented in fifty-cent or dollar groups, annual incomes or earnings, in one-hundred-dollar groups, at least until $1,500 is reached. Only thus can *distribution* be shown.

In the presentation of income statistics, the time unit causes no small difficulty. The smallest period that can be considered economically complete is the year, for only the annual unit is unaffected by the succession of seasons which is so vitally connected with agriculture, lumbering, fishing, canning, rice cleaning and polishing, ice manufacture, millinery, and a host of other industries. Moreover, salaries are expressed in terms of the year. By the use of no other than the twelve-month unit can the factor of unemployment be adequately taken into account. As has been pointed out, however, incompetence, carelessness, and unwillingness of individuals in answering questions, coupled with the difficulty of following one person through many pay rolls are great obstacles to the practical application of the annual unit. It must be admitted, on the other hand, that in 1901, the Bureau of Labor actually did procure apparently reliable returns of the annual incomes of over twenty-five thousand families.[1]

[1] See the *Eighteenth Annual Report of the Commissioner of Labor, Wages and the Cost of Living.*

The natural pay time-unit seems to be the week, and it is the weekly rate, or the actual weekly wage which is most easily procured from the pay rolls. If the rate of pay is presented, as in the *Dewey Report,* the reader is not told what actual earnings are, but if the earnings are published the returns cannot be exactly interpreted without a knowledge of how many individuals have been shifted from one group to another by the lost days or over-time which may have been peculiar to their particular establishment in that week. From this dilemma the *Census of Manufactures* of 1905 seeks escape by recording actual earnings for the "busy week" or week of largest employment in each establishment. Even this expedient is open to some objection, as in the busy week, there may have been employed an unusually large proportion of comparatively inexperienced and unskilled hands; this would tend to swell the lower wage groups; but on the other hand, there would probably be an unusual amount of over-time in this period. The selection of a "normal" week is probably one which secures the closest approximation to true representation of the distribution of earnings. This *á priori* discussion cannot settle the point; it may make little practical difference whether the busy, the normal, or a certain week arbitrarily fixed by the calendar is selected. Only experiment will afford the answer; but this much is certain and important—whether rates or earnings be tabulated, weekly pay is a very uncertain guide to annual incomes from labor.[1]

Another point at which the ideal and the possible conflict is in the choice of the unit of labor. It seems vital to know the facts about family incomes, but for this purpose

[1] Hourly and daily rates or earnings, provided they are accompanied by the hours of labor per day and per week, will usually lead to substantially the same results and are of course subject to the same limitations as weekly figures.

the earnings of individuals are of little value. It is also desirable to know how many mature men are able, without the aid of wives and children, decently to support their families. For this purpose weekly figures fail, and the Census division between men and boys at the sixteenth birthday is futile.

In view of all these difficulties the claim of any feasible statistics of income to be called " ideal " must be advanced with modesty. In the first place, ideal income statistics would be separately tabulated for the urban and rural portions of each state or group of states, and would be supplemented by corresponding data on the costs and standards of living, or on the purchasing power of money. The families of each locality would be grouped by total annual income in classes of one hundred dollars, at least until the fifteen-hundred-dollar mark was reached and preferably as far as two thousand dollars; from that point five-hundred-dollar groups would suffice. Each income group would be again subdivided according to sources: is the revenue derived from the ownership of property, from the earnings of the family's head,[1] from the earnings of the head increased by wages of other members of the household, from the ownership of property combined with the earnings of the head, or from property and earnings of the head and other family members? Another classification would divide men of at least twenty-one years according to earnings, occupation, residence, and race. The data would be collected by expert special agents, in a house-to-house visitation, all doubtful returns being ruthlessly discarded.

The funds being unavailable for so elaborate a study, the weekly wage rates of men of voting age might be drawn from the pay rolls of as many employers as possible. Names

---

[1] By head is meant here the earner of the largest wages.

of men, selected in considerable numbers from each occupation, would be made the basis of a canvass for further facts concerning the amount and sources of the total family income and the amount of unemployment during the year. A special investigation would have to be made into the incomes of farm families, of fatherless households, and of as many employers and business men as would submit to the "inquisition". The results would establish with more or less accuracy the relations between wage rates and annual earnings for the different occupations, and between wage rates and family incomes, and from these relations the distribution of incomes among families might be approximated. In order to make this estimate possible, however, the distribution of family incomes among the men of *each wage group* would have to be shown.

Either one of these studies would fall short of the ideal: the first because it would be impossible to obtain the necessary data from a large group of fairly well-to-do and prosperous families, the second because it would depend so largely upon estimate. Yet either method would probably afford a sufficient foundation for the discussion of the problems outlined in the first chapter.

CHAPTER III

Sources of Incomes

As is the case with many economic terms, the best meaning of " income " is a matter of dispute. The income of an individual may be defined psychologically as a sum of enjoyments available in a unit of time. Impossible it may be at present to measure "pleasures and pains"; yet the fact that increases in the rates of wages among certain groups of the population are regularly followed by augmented voluntary idleness, makes the " enjoyment " idea of real importance to the economist. Even if the scope of the word be limited to material things, there is no final agreement. Suppose, for example, that in the course of the year 1912 Mr. A buys on various days fifty city lots at an aggregate cost of $75,-000, and subsequently sells them for a total price of $100,-000. He may have begun the year with $30,000 and ended it with $55,000, yet to the minds of some scientists his income was $100,000, of which he spent a large proportion. Others would hold that Mr. A's income was $25,000, or $25,000 minus the cost of carrying on the business. In view of these differences of definition, it is necessary to state that, for the purposes of this essay, the income of an individual is the aggregate of economic goods which in the course of a unit of time become available to him for final consumption without entailing impairment of his capital. Unless otherwise stated, the time unit is the year, and the income is expressed in terms of money. So defined, personal incomes are derived from three sources: from LABOR, from the OWNERSHIP OF PROPERTY, and from the RIGHTS OF PRIVATE PROPERTY.

"Labor is a wealth-creating effort."[1] Any human exertion directed primarily toward the creation of utility is labor. Although the work of a child at school may create "productive power", the immediate end not being production, it is not economic labor. "The remuneration of labor,"[2] "the earnings assigned to men for their work,"[3] in other words, the recompense of human exertion in the production of utility is wages. Thus in the economic sense wages includes more than is popularly understood by the term, includes *all* material incomes which reward labor. Theoretically every one of the thirty million Americans engaged in gainful occupations either actually receives or should impute to himself wages. The salary of the president of the United States Steel Corporation, the profit of the underwriter, and the pay of the laborer fall in the same category. These examples, however, illustrate the three varieties of wages.

Perhaps it would be better to say that there are two classes of wages, one of which may be subdivided. In the first place, the amount of remuneration may be determined in advance by definite agreement. Such a stipend is a salary if the contract is for a year or more, wages (in the popular sense) if the time unit is less than twelve months.[4] Although, perhaps, not strictly included by the definition, what are generally known as piece payments are rightly classed with wages proper for two reasons: first, the piece rate is usually determined in the beginning by what a normal oper-

[1] J. B. Clark, *Essentials of Economic Theory*, p. 9.
[2] Seligman, *Principles of Economics*, p. 411.
[3] Seager, *Introduction to Economics*, p. 222.
[4] *Abstract of the Twelfth Census*, p. 300, note 2.

ative produces in a given period, and is frequently reduced
if this standard is much exceeded : [1] second, the tasks of the
piece worker, and his social position correspond very closely
to those of the time worker. The other class of rewards of
labor includes those forms of compensation which depend
in a peculiar degree upon the skill, energy, and good fortune
of the recipient. Under this head would fall, for example,
the commissions of salesmen and of brokers, the " profits "
of the farmer and shop-keeper (except interest on capital),
the incomes of physicians and lawyers, and a large part of
the speculator's gain. Although there seems to be no recognized name for this group of indeterminate remunerations,
for convenience, and without essential inaccuracy, it may be
styled " contingent earnings ". The income of a particular
individual may vary but little from year to year and still be
in a proper sense " contingent ". This distinction is by no
means fanciful, for, in addition to the economic significance,
there are corresponding lines of social cleavage. In society
the salaried man seems to occupy a higher position than the
wage earner, regardless of the comparative size of their incomes ; in the four hundreds, are the families enjoying contingent earnings. Doubtless this social gradation is partly
due to the distribution of property : the wage-worker is
seldom a large owner, the salaried person may not possess
property but often does, and a prime requisite for the enjoyment of a contingent income is frequently the control of
some capital.

That one man may procure labor incomes of all three
classes should require no explanation. A professor, for instance, may be paid a salary for teaching, he may be given
a weekly wage for summer work in a government bureau,
and may in addition be blessed with large checks for scien-

[1] Adams and Sumner, *Labor Problems*, p. 264; *Twelfth Census, Employees and Wages*, p. xix.

tific articles, or fees as a consulting expert. Thus one person may receive a salary, wages, and a contingent income.

Recognizing, then, this demarkation of the rewards of labor into wages, salaries, and contingent earnings, the question of the relative importance of these groups arises. Although no attempt has ever been made in the United States to gather statistics upon the basis of such a classification, an approximation may be obtained from the data in the *Census of Occupations* and in the *Census of Manufactures.* The latter distinguishes between " firm members ", " salaried employees ", and " wage-earners ". In the light of this information, and of a general knowledge of the modes of remuneration in the various branches of industry it is possible to form a rough table.

TABLE I

CLASSIFICATION OF RECIPIENTS OF INCOMES FROM LABOR IN THE
UNITED STATES, 1900

I.	II.	III.	IV.
Division of industry.	Wages.	Salaries.	Contingent earnings.
Agricultural pursuits	4,863,000	18,000	5,557,000
Professional service	6,000	819,000	440,000
Domestic and personal service . .	5,154,000	131,000	409,000
Trade and transportation . . .	2,317,000	1,079,000	1,382,000
Manufacturing [1] and mechanical . .	6,001,000	403,000	709,000
Totals	18,341,000	2,450,000	8,497,000

From this it would appear that, of the twenty-nine million

_____

[1] Proprietors and firm members, 708,623; salaried officials, clerks, etc., 397,092; wage-earners (average number), 5,314,539. *Abstract of the Twelfth Census*, p. 300.

persons gainfully employed in 1900, about six-tenths were wage-earners, nearly one-tenth were on salaries, and approximately three-tenths enjoyed contingent incomes.[1]

In this connection it is interesting to note that the salary seems to be gaining in favor over the wage as a form of remuneration. In 1899, the factories employed 5,079,225 persons, of whom 7.15 per cent were on salaries; in 1904, 5,990,072, 8.68 per cent being on salaries; in 1909, 7,405,-313, with 10.67 per cent salaried. Perhaps the magnitude of this change is made more apparent if it is stated thus: in 1899, the factories employed one salaried person to every 12.9 wage earners; in 1904, one to every 10.5; in 1909, one to every 8.4.[2] Table II shows that so far as the facts are revealed by published data this movement toward the salary as a form of remuneration is general. Whatever may be the significance of this tendency, one inference can be drawn with some degree of assurance; an increase in the proportion of workers who receive salaries means an increase of the proportion of the employed class who, being able to count on a definite annual income, do not need to dread recurring periods of unemployment.

The second source of income is the ownership of property. The yield of lands and houses, the return from capital—whether invested in mortgages, bonds, stocks, partnerships, or individual businesses—royalties, and other less important forms of revenue, in fact all that the Economist calls rent, interest, and profits, are included in this class. Profits belong to the owner of a business, whether or not he owns the capital or manages the concern. In its pure form,

---

[1] It is interesting to note the rough agreement between these results and the estimate of Professor Seager—employing class, 9,830,000; employed class, 19,100,000.

[2] *Thirteenth Census Bulletin Manufactures: United States,* p. 3. Table II of this essay also.

TABLE II

RATIOS OF SALARIED EMPLOYEES TO WAGE-EARNERS IN CERTAIN INDUSTRIES

I.	II.	III.	IV.	V.	VI.	VII.	VIII.	IX.
	Earlier period.		Later period.		Per cent of employees on salary.		Number of wage-earners to one salaried employee.	
Industry.	Salaried employees.	Wage-earners.	Salaried employees.	Wage-earners.	Earlier period.	Later period.	Earlier period.	Later period.
1. Street railways . . .	7,128	133,641	11,700	209,729	5.06	5.28	18.7	17.9
2. Electric light and power plants . . .	6,096	23,330	12,090	34,642	23.07	27.27	3.3	2.7
3. Telephones	14,124	64,628	25,298	118,871	18.14	17.55	4.6	4.7
4. Telegraphs	337	14,591	829	26,798	2.27	3.00	43.3	32.3
5. Manufactures . . .	364,202	4,715,023	519,751	5,470,321	7.15	8.68	12.9	10.5

References, Special Census Reports:

1. *Street and Electric Railways*, 1907, p. 193. Figures for 1902 and 1907.
2. *Central Electric Light and Power Stations*, 1907, p. 92. Figures for 1902 and 1907.
3. *The Telephone Industry*, 1907, p. 71. Figures for 1902 and 1907.
4. *Telephones and Telegraphs*, 1902, pp. 99, 102. Figures for 1880 and 1902.
5. *Manufactures*, 1905, vol. i, p. lxxi. Figures for 1899 and 1904.

In 1909 the factories in continental United States employed 790,267 persons on salaries and 6,615,046 on wages. Thus 10.67 per cent of the employees were salaried and there were 8.4 wage-earners to one salaried employee.

income from property ownership accrues, for example, to
one whose fortune consists of stocks and long-term bonds,
one who receives dividends and interest without the necessity of reinvesting; or to a person who leaves the adminis-
tration of his wealth entirely in the hands of an agent,
trustee, or attorney. If, however, the individual speculates
on the exchange, rents his own houses, purchases short-time
mortgages, tills his farm, or conducts his store, then his income is derived from two sources, labor and the ownership
of property. However clever he may be, without the control of property, the speculator can not carry on his business, and so, although his skill enormously increases his
earnings, they are due in part to capital, are not pure economic wages. There seems to be a considerable number of
men, who, with a small sum of, say, ten thousand dollars,
by devoting their entire time to the stock market, extract
annual incomes of an approximately equal amount. By
way of contrast, it is not an extremely infrequent phenom-
enon for the proprietor of a business to continue year after
year with a net income less than his capital would earn if
otherwise safely invested. His wages are either negative,
or else they are entirely psychological and consist of the
pleasure of being an *entrepreneur;* considering the situation
from another viewpoint, his wages are ample, but his investment bears scant interest. Thus it is apparent how difficult may be the attempt to distinguish between income from
the ownership of property and income from labor: in practice they are frequently inseparable.

How many American citizens own property is a question
that defies statistical answer. It is, however, possible to
present some facts in regard to holdings of real estate and
of corporation securities. The Census of 1900 shows that,
of the 10,488,814 families not on farms, 2,338,533, or 23.4
per cent, owned their own homes clear of encumbrance;

1,101,802, or 12.9 per cent, lived in mortgaged houses to which they held title; and the remaining 6,351,836 hired their dwellings.[1] That a large proportion of the non-rural families do not possess real estate, is, therefore, perfectly clear, but to the actual number of owners of these six million hired tenements, no clue is evident. Again, in 1900, there were 5,739,657 farms, of which 3,654,158 were occupied by owners and part owners, over a million being mortgaged. Hired managers cultivated 59,213 farms, and the other 2,026,286 were rented.[2] The ownership of 95.5 per cent of these rented farms could be traced, and it was found that their titles were held by 1,257,716 individuals.[3] Since seventy-five per cent of the rented farms were in the county of the owners' residence, it is highly probable that many of these landlords lived upon other farms which they owned. It may therefore be concluded that there were not more than five million nor less than thirty-six hundred thousand title holders of the 5,739,657 American farms.[4] Uncertain as these figures are, they become still more vague when the mortgage complication is introduced. Thus, the number

---

[1] *Abstract of the Twelfth Census*, p. 28.

[2] *Twelfth Census of the United States, vol. v, Agriculture*, pt. i, p. lxvi. The *Advance Statement of General Agricultural Data*, issued by Director Durand of the Census Bureau in September, 1911, shows that of the 6,340,357 farms in 1910, 3,933,705 were worked by the owners, 1,311,364 being mortgaged; 2,349,254 were held by tenants, and 57,398 were in charge of managers. Thus the per cent of farms held by tenants had increased from 35.3 in 1900 to 37.1 in 1910. During the same period it seems that the per cent of mortgaged farms among those inhabited by owners increased from about 30.4 to 33.3.

[3] *Twelfth Census of the United States, vol. v, Agriculture*, pt. i, p. lxxxvii.

[4] For strict accuracy this number should be increased by about 451,-515, the number of part owners on farms, making the maximum 5,450,-000 owners.

of owners of real estate can not even be guessed. And
were this number known, a new problem would arise
in determining how many put their land to productive
uses, for there are persons who are " land poor ", others
own parks, or run expensive dilletanti farms, and there are
always vacant houses. Even to approximate the number of
persons deriving incomes from the ownership of real prop-
perty, is, therefore, impossible.

If the distribution of ownership of real estate is hidden,
what of industrial capital? *The Wall Street Journal* of 31
August, 1911, presented a list of some 242 railroad and industrial corporations, giving for each the par value of the
outstanding capital stock, the number of shares, the number of shareholders, and the average number of shares per
stockowner, at the closing of the books nearest to July 1,
1901, 1906, and 1911. These figures are summarized as
follows:

TABLE III

HOLDINGS OF STOCK IN INDUSTRIAL AND RAILWAY CORPORATIONS, 1901–1911

I.	II.	III.	IV.
	1911.	1906.	1901.
Capitalization (stock)	$8,997,347,426	$7,323,147,307	$5,559,275,316
Shares	110,426,197	86,636,251	60,254,988
Shareholders	872,392	394,842	226,480
Average shares per holder	126.5	219.4	266.1
Average par value of stock per holder	$10,313	$18,547	$24,546

Among other interesting deductions, the *Wall Street
Journal* maintains the following:

1. Only a little more than $10,000 par value is in the hands

of each holder, or in the terms of shares of stock which aggre-
gated about 110,000,000, less than 130 shares to each average
holder.

2. Broadly speaking, despite the growing capitalization,
stocks are receiving larger distribution year by year. The unit
shareholder owns a smaller amount to-day than five years ago,
and a still smaller one as compared with 1901. Corporations,
in other words, are owned not by the great financiers, but by the
100-share men, the owners of $10,000 worth of stock each.

3. What an army of shareholders is summed up in 870,000
holders from 242 reporting companies!

It must be recognized that, in preparing this table, the
Wall Street Journal has rendered a valuable service. There
is no apparent ground for doubting the soundness of many
of the writer's conclusions, but some of his assertions are
so worded as to make upon the casual reader an impression
which the figures certainly do not warrant. Among these
doubtful propositions are the three quoted.

In the first place, the sum of the numbers of stockholders
in the several corporations is not necessarily the number of
individuals who own the stock. For example, the shares of the
United States Steel Corporation were owned by one hundred
twenty thousand persons, and those of the Pennsylvania
Railroad by sixty-nine thousand. Is it possible that there
were no individuals who were investors in both of these
companies? One does not have to seek very far in some
parts of New York City in order to find men who are interested in several corporations! It is, indeed, mathemati-
cally possible that the one hundred twenty thousand owners
of the "Steel Trust" were also the owners of the entire two
hundred forty-two concerns on the list.[1]

---

[1] The writer for the *Wall Street Journal* ignores the great importance
of inter-corporate holdings. The *Special Report of the Census Bureau*

The true number of individuals actually holding the stock of these companies could be discovered only by eliminating duplications through a comparison of the *names* on the registry books. As an illustration of the possible import of this criticism, it may be illuminating to cite the case of the Standard Oil Company. In July, 1911, according to the *Wall Street Journal,* this company had a capital stock of $98,388,300, divided among 6,101 persons. Since that time, the corporation has been dissolved into thirty-three companies, each shareholder receiving a proportionate amount of stock in each concern. Thus, supposing no sales to have taken place, if the article were being written to-day,

on the Express Companies, 1907 (pp. 19, 20), shows the following holdings by express companies:

EXPRESS COMPANY HOLDINGS OF RAILWAY AND EXPRESS COMPANY SECURITIES, 1907

I.	II.	III.	IV.
Express company.	Railway stock.	Railway bonds.	Express stock.
Adams.....................	$13,865,650	$902,000	$3,295,925
American	8,002,800	6,730,000	2,546,400
Northern..................	100,000	....	5,000,000
Southern..................	55,000	215,000	300,300
United States	195,500	3,454,000	56,200
International	....	....	345,000
Wells Fargo	....	1,001,000	74,300
Globe	....	22,000	....
Total	$22,218,950	$12,324,000	$11,618,125

Total holdings of stock, $33,837,075 par value.

On the other hand, the railways held, June 30, 1906, $20,668,000 of express company stock (p. 19).

Of the $18,417,132,238 outstanding railway securities June 30, 1910, $5,100,814,274 was held by railway corporations. *Statistics of the Railroads,* 1910, p. 52.

the total number of shareholders would be 201,333. This change, hidden among the statistics of other companies, the *Wall Street Journal* would herald as a remarkable diffusion of ownership. It is not intended to intimate that the writer in question could perpetrate so obvious a fallacy; yet to an analogous error, more serious because better concealed, he has certainly fallen victim. What is the average holding of a shareholder in these two hundred and forty-two corporations? $10,313? The data do not warrant the conclusion. How many shareholders are in this army? It is impossible to say at present; surely less than 872,392.

Perhaps further criticism is unnecessary, but clearness may be gained by a consideration of the extent of that change of distribution of ownership claimed in the second of the quoted conclusions. In 1901, according to the table, the corporations reported outstanding stock of a par value of $5,559,275,316, in the hands of 226,480 shareholders. Now in this total of over five and a half billions, is included $1,461,709,545, the capitalization of thirty-eight companies which failed to make public the numbers of their shareholders. For three companies, owned by 5,215 persons, the capital was not recorded. Correcting for these two errors of opposite tendency, it appears that the average block in those corporations which reported both items was $18,519, $6,027 less than the $24,546 of the table. Likewise in the totals for 1911 are included 11,154 stockholders the aggregate value of whose interests is not given, and $12,905,200, the capital of concerns not numbering their owners. These corrections raise the average holdings by $119, to $10,432. Thus, whereas the reduction of the average block according to the figures of the *Wall Street Journal* was $14,233, or fifty-eight per cent of $24,546, the actual diminution was $8,087, or forty-four per cent of $18,519. The *Journal's* figures, therefore, exaggerate the rate of decrease by over thirty per cent and the absolute reduction by seventy-five per cent.[1]

It appears, therefore, that any conclusions as to the num-

[1] Suppose there actually were 872,000 individual stockowners in these corporations, what is the distribution of holdings among them? In 1880, 42,262 men owned $327,185,500 in government bonds, an average of nearly $8,000. However, 13,309 of these men owned an aggregate of but $4,067,050—an average of $306; and 830 held $176,239,350—an average of over $212,000. In other words, two per cent of the male bondholders owned over half the bonds held by men. The details are as follows:

HOLDERS OF REGISTERED UNITED STATES BONDS, 1880

I.	II.	III.	IV.	V.	VI.	VII.
	Number of holders.			Amount of holdings by		
Size of holding.	Males.	Females.	Corporations.	Males.	Females.	Corporations.
$50,000–over	830	168	531	$176,239,350	$23,344,900	$210,695,150
25,000–$50,000..	1,018	281	224	38,668,100	10,747,850	9,314,650
10,000– 25,000..	2,326	953	259	38,861,750	15,395,600	4,886,500
5,000– 10,000..	3,416	1,571	196	27,090,900	12,235,400	1,753,600
2,500– 5,000..	5,490	2,861	149	21,406,300	11,032,950	631,700
1,000– 2,500..	7,505	4,871	53	13,402,300	8,532,850	97,400
500– 1,000..	8,368	6,372	59	7,449,750	5,591,100	56,400
50– 500..	13,309	12,248	56	4,067,050	3,472,700	16,150
Totals	42,262	29,325	1,527	$327,185,500	$90,353,350	$227,451,550

Tenth Census of the United States, Public Indebtedness, p. 235. The United States Steel Corporation and the International Paper Company have been selling stock on easy terms to their employees. Such a policy might largely increase the number of stockholders and decrease the average block without in the slightest impairing or altering the size of the blocks owned by individuals at the inauguration of the plan. Thus conclusions based on these averages are particularly illusory.

ber of persons in the United States deriving incomes from the ownership of property, real or industrial, must be based more upon speculation than upon facts. It is not denied that the ownership of stock companies may be in a process of diffusion; the simple fact is that the magnitude of this extension, the character of the distribution is not known.[1]

Incomes of the third class are neither the rewards of labor, nor the returns to the owner of productive property. For want of a better term, they may be said to arise from the RIGHT OF PRIVATE PROPERTY; they include, mainly, gifts, bequests, and inheritances. " That the inheritance is an income to him who secures it there can be no doubt." [2]   A peculiarity of income from the right of private property is that it is not normally a part of the distribution of products, but is rather a transfer of the ownership of capital. In a completely socialized state, whether or not interest were legally abolished, there would still be incomes from labor, and income from capital; but there would be no incomes from the right of private property—save perhaps small inheritances of personal effects. Incomes from the right of private property differ from such windfalls as speculative

---

[1] In 1904 the total stock of the American Railways, $6,339,899,329 (*Statistical Abstract of the United States*, 1908, p. 256), was owned in 327,851 blocks. According to the 1911 figures of the *Wall Street Journal*, about forty railways with a stock issue of $3,658,760,390 were owned in 290,145 blocks. The eighteen railway companies reporting stock lists in 1901 and 1911 show a total of 61,961 holders at the earlier, and 138,406 at the later date. Probably greater diffusion of ownership plays some part in this enormous increase, yet the warning of Martin A. Knapp must not be forgotten: " It cannot, however, be said that this figure (327,851) accurately represents the number of individuals interested in railway securities. . . . To the extent to which the same individual is an investor in the ·stock of more than one company, the above figure includes duplications." *Sen. Doc.* no. 188, 58th Cong., 3d Ses.

[2] H. C. Adams, *Finance*, p. 360.

profits in that, except in such cases as those involving the
capture of affections, they do not as a rule presuppose the
element of shrewdness or the control of capital.   Although
the sum of inheritances in the United States in any one year
must be considerable, it is not a great factor in the nature
of the distribution of regular incomes in this sense, that the
inheritance is, if large, normally a transfer between individuals of an income from property ownership.

The importance of these incomes from the right of
private property is better known abroad than it is in the
United States.   During the years 1903 to 1907, among the
French population of approximately 38,333,000, there were
annually about 780,000 deaths, an average of 356,310, over
forty-five per cent, of these decedents leaving estates of one
franc or more.   Nineteen per cent (148,556) of those who
died were possessed of property worth not less than £100.
In England, by way of contrast, but nine and four-tenths
per cent of the 546,000 decedents left estates valued as high
as £100.[1]   A curious custom in France is that of the father
handing over property to his son some time before death
(donations) ; in the course of the year these gifts have
amounted to one-seventh, and at times almost to a fourth
of the inheritances.[2]   Only three and eight-tenths per cent
of the decedents in England leave property to the amount
of £1,000 or over.   The following table gives interesting
details of inheritances in France and England.

[1] *Journal of the Royal Statistical Society*, June, 1910, vol. 73, p. 636.
[2] *Ibid.*, 1893, vol. 56, p. 600.

TABLE IV

CLASSIFICATION OF INHERITANCES IN FRANCE AND ENGLAND

(Figures are the arithmetic means of the figures for the years 1903, 1904, 1905, 1907)

France.

Estate Exceeding—But not exceeding	Number of estates.	Per cent of estates.	Value of estates. £	Per cent of value.
£ 100 400	89,877	60.50	19,365,081	9.40
400 2,000	43,978	29.60	37,496,041	18.20
2,000 4,000	7,194	4.84	20,010,126	9.72
4,000 10,000	4,632	3.12	28,856,271	14
10,000 20,000	1,601	1.08	22,587,889	10.96
20,000 40,000	765	.51	21,353,912	10.36
40,000 80,000	338	.23	19,095,000	9.27
80,000 200,000	131	.09	15,418,872	7.49
200,000 400,000	29	.02	8,327,896	4.04
400,000 2,000,000	9.25	.01	6,781,249	3.29
Over 2,000,000	1.75	....	6,747,329	3.27
Totals	148,556	100	206,059,566	100

England.

Estate Exceeding—But not exceeding	Estates. Number.	Per cent.	Value of estates. £	Per cent.
£ 100 500	33,061.75	52.17	9,947,533	3.56
500 1,000	10,322.5	15.86	8,554,683	3.06
1,000 10,000	16,822	25.84	61,550,267	22.02
10,000 25,000	2,340.75	3.60	41,252,699	14.76
25,000 50,000	907.75	1.40	35,363,725	12.65
50,000 75,000	285.25	.44	19,437,164	6.96
75,000 100,000	142.75	.22	13,093,382	4.69
100,000 150,000	132.25	.20	16,949,494	6.06
150,000 250,000	93.75	.14	20,324,934	7.27
250,000 500,000	55.75	.09	20,718,998	7.41
500,000 1,000,000	19.75	.03	14,961,037	5.35
Over 1,000,000	6.5	.01	17,351,706	6.21
Totals	65,094.5	100	279,507,622	100

Possibly because of the blessings of decentralized government, the United States has no general inheritance tax. Although several of the commonwealths have instituted such duties, but few classified returns are available. In the aggregate value of property, New York is certainly the richest of the states, and her per capita wealth is surpassed probably only in the District of Columbia, Nebraska, Montana, Wyoming, Colorado, Arizona, Nevada, Oregon, and California.[1] Between 1904 and 1908, the average annual number of deaths in New York was about 141,000, and the mean number of estates taxed as being worth $5,000 or more was 5,900; thus about four per cent of the decedents in the Empire State leave property worth as much as $5,000. Of the 138,883 persons who died in 1908, 47,202 were males over twenty-five years of age.[2] In that year 6,233 estates were taxed. Thus, in one of the richest commonwealths in the Union only one man in eight dies worth $5,000. Further than this it is impossible to go, as no record is kept of the total values of all the estates taxed.

There are, then, three sources of income, labor, the ownership of property, and the right of private property. Incomes from labor, the rewards of personal exertion, may be subdivided into three classes, salaries which are enjoyed by about one-tenth of the gainfully employed, wages which are earned by approximately six-tenths, and contingent incomes which accrue to the remaining three-tenths. Among the employed, the salary seems to be gaining over the wage

---

[1] *Census, Weealth, Debt, and Taxation*, 1904. pp. 42, 44.

[2] Calculated from figures in *Mortality Statistics*, 1908, *Bureau of the Census*, pp. 368, 454; see also pp. 103. 120. From the *Reports of the Comptroller of the State of New York*, it appears that the number of estates taxed in 1905 was 5,431; in 1906, 5,881; in 1907, 6,041, and in 1908, 6,233—average, 5,897. After 1908 only the number of appraisals is given; not all appraisals result in a tax. *Reports*, 1906. p. xlii; 1908, p. xlix; 1909, p. xxxii.

as the preferred method of remuneration. A determination of the number of persons enjoying incomes from property is impossible on the basis of existing data; it is not known how many persons are interested in real estate, how many are holders of industrial or railroad stocks, or how many own United States bonds. Finally, for the last three years not even the aggregate value of the estates of at least $5,000 actually taxed in New York has been made available. It is therefore apparent that the people of the United States are in profound ignorance of the sources from which they derive their incomes.[1]

[1] Dr. Spahr, in his *Essay on the Present Distribution of Wealth in the United States*, pp. 88-92, 120, has concluded that in Basel, France, Saxony, the United Kingdom, and the United States, forty per cent of the national income goes to capital and sixty per cent to labor. Recent available figures for eight large American industries, employing over three million laborers, give to capital a return in dividends and interest of $1,276,419,050, and to labor in salaries and wages of $2,031,402,210, a total income of $3,307,821,260, of which the share of labor is sixty-one per cent, and that of capital thirty-nine per cent. That these figures are typical of the whole field of American industry is questionable.

RETURNS OF CAPITAL AND LABOR IN EIGHT INDUSTRIES

I.	II.	III.	IV.	V.	VI.
Industry.	Year	Outstanding capital stock and bonds. $	Interest and dividends. $	Wages and Salaries. $	Employees.
1. Telegraphs	1902	162,946,525	8,206,975	15,030,673	27,627
2. Telephones	1907	1,072,805,993	36,049,779	68,279,127	144,169
3. Express companies.	1910	105,523,300	33,564,411	39,491,032	79,284
4. Central electric light and power stations	1907	1,341,995,182	46,142,902	31,935,309	42,066
5. Street and electric railways	1907	3,774,772,096	125,954,062	150,991,099	221,429
6. Incorporated mines and quarries	1902	3,217,719,458	86,020,837	354,079,476	528,720
7. 185 industrial combinations	1900	3,093,095,868	135,126,612	227,861,188	424,686
8. Steam railways	1910	18,417,132,238	805,353,472	1,143,725,306	1,699,420
Totals	......	31,185,990,660	1,276,419,050	2,031,402,210	3,167,401

References—Special Census Reports:

1. *Telephones and Telegraphs,* 1902, p. 99.

2. *Telephones,* 1907, pp. 57, 59, 71.

3. Interstate Commerce Commission, *Report on Statistics of Express Companies* for year ending June 30, 1910, pp. 15, 30. The dividends are abnormal, including a $24,000,000 dividend by the Wells Fargo Company (capital $12,000,000)—wages and salaries, and number of employees from *Census Bulletin, Express Business in the United States,* 1907, pp. 14, 15.

4. *Central Elec. Light and Power Stations,* 1907, pp. 61, 89, 92 (commercial).

5. *Street and Electric Railways,* 1907, pp. 97, 193.

6. *Mines and Quarries,* 1902, pp. 88, 68, 72.

7. *Manufactures,* 1900, pt. ii, pp. lxxix-lxxxvi (interest of $216,412,-759 worth of bonds not reported).

8. *Statistics of the Railways,* 1910, pp. 33, 44, 50, 51, 55, 57.

CHAPTER IV

The Sources of American Income Statistics

SINCE, as was shown in the previous chapter, not even the number of persons enjoying incomes from the ownership of property and from the right of private property is known, it is presumptuous to expect to find any figures of the distribution of these revenues. The rewards of labor, on the other hand, have long attracted the attention of the statisticians. American statistics of annual incomes, it is true, are scanty enough, but a great mass of wage data has been published by the state bureaus of labor and by the Federal Government.

A detailed description of these state reports is unnecessary, but it may be well to point out just what material they offer to the serious investigator of the distribution of incomes. It must constantly be borne in mind, that in the various commonwealths the purposes of these bureaus are very different. For example, judging simply by their reports, some of the states, especially in the west, conceive of a labor or industrial commission as an advertising agency, the prime purpose of which is to attract immigration of men and capital. The natural result of such a concept is the publication of some photographs of genuine artistic merit, and a series of vague, but glowing, generalizations, printed in beautiful type and supported by a few figures apparently conjured out of the air, or deduced by introspection. Other states devote their energies largely to studying the " industrial opportunities " in each town or county, to

a manufacturing or labor " chronology ", to directories of
organizations, to studies of accidents in factories and mines,
to attempts at conciliation in labor disputes, to special investigations resulting in monographs, or to the compilation
of various classes of industrial data.   Indeed, one un-
familiar with them would be surprised at the multi-form
activities of the state bureaus of labor.   The reports of
Massachusetts, New Jersey, New York, Wisconsin, and
Illinois in particular abound in valuable articles on special
subjects.   Therefore to condemn the reports of the majority of the state labor departments, simply because
they contain no adequate wage data, would be rank in-
justice: what follows relates only to their offering of material to aid in a study of incomes.   However, it can in fair-
ness be said that in very few states have there been exhibited
both an appreciation of the importance of collecting such
statistics and a knowledge of valuable methods of gathering and presenting them.   In none has there been made an
extensive study of annual incomes.

Rather limited compilations of yearly incomes and earnings, however, have until recently, been made annually in
Kansas and biennially in Iowa.[1]   In the labor reports of
these states have been incorporated the complete individual
replies to an elaborate questionnaire sent out to working
men of many occupations, including even "clerks ".   Among
the questions is one calling for the total earnings during
the year, in Kansas, income also, and another asking
whether the worker has a family dependent upon him for
support.   These data have much to commend them.   First,
from the individual returns the investigator can make any
tabulation he finds useful.   Second, the earnings for a year
being given, the allowance for unemployment is automati-

---

[1] 1907 is the last year for which Kansas compiled these statistics.

cally made. Third, the same system has been followed for
a series of years, thus allowing some estimate of the short-
time trend of wages. Fourth, the replies are from mature
men, nearly all of whom are heads of families: this is a decided advantage over so many statistical presentations
wherein all males over sixteen or over twenty years of age
are included in the same tabulation. Fifth, the data cover
occupations but scantily touched, if at all in the other compilations of wage statistics, which are so frequently confined to manufactures; and in addition the studies are state-
wide. There is, therefore, much to commend this part of
the work of the Kansas and Iowa Bureaus of Labor, but
there are some countervailing weaknesses: First, four or
five hundred cases is a rather small sample to be surely
representative of the conditions even in a thinly-populated
state. Second, as about twenty occupations are included,
the number in each must be quite limited. Third, the returns are almost universally from members of trade-unions,
and cannot, therefore, be used to shed any light upon the
condition of non-union men, or of workers "in general".
Fourth, it is not improbable that the men who have the
ability and the interest to fill out such long blanks, are
rather above the "average" in intelligence and consequently in earning power. Fifth, it is sometimes questioned whether any workmen are capable of accurately answering questions regarding their financial status. But this
danger can hardly be considered serious, for although it is
difficult to "keep accounts", absolute exactness of the individual returns is not a necessity to good statistics; it is
probable that the errors are at least partially compensating,
and, if his pay is small, a man is not likely to make a very
large mistake in estimating his earnings. In brief, then,
these two states furnish data which, if used with care, are
of considerable value.

For the sake of completeness, three recent studies should be mentioned. The report of the Wisconsin Bureau of Labor Statistics for 1907-1908 gives the classified incomes of eighty-two families, female members of which were employed in the Milwaukee tanneries. The 1906 and 1908 reports of the Illinois Bureau of Labor contain the results of searching investigations among the women employed in factories and in department stores. For those women whose names appeared on fifty or more weekly pay rolls, the total earnings during the year are given, individually, and in classified tables. A large number of individuals is included in each case, and there is good ground for believing that the statistics are truly typical. The number of girls in the department stores whose wages are given is 2,556, but the annual earnings of only 1,660 are presented.[1] What were the incomes of the other 896? Their case is just as interesting as that of the full-time workers; whether the unemployment was voluntary or involuntary, their problems are doubtless more acute. The income of the person who is steadily employed can be determined just as well from the weekly as from the yearly earnings; in order to estimate the welfare of those who suffer from idleness, their annual incomes must be known. This should not be construed as adverse criticism of the excellent report under discussion, it is merely evidence that the most-needed information is hardest to obtain. It seems, then, that a search through the state publications for statistics of annual incomes, or family earnings is fruitless so far as results of general applicability are concerned; but in certain limited fields, Kansas, Iowa, Illinois, and Wisconsin offer valuable material.

If annual earnings have not been tabulated, there are still large possibilities in the statistics of classified wages. These

---

[1] *Biennial Report, Bureau of Labor Statistics, Illinois*, 1908, pp. 426, 445.

are regularly furnished by four states. The Wisconsin Bureau of Labor early undertook a regular publication of such figures; Massachusetts adopted the plan the very same year, 1889, New Jersey in 1896, and Kansas in 1900. All four of these commonwealths still furnish these annual tables of classified wages of the employees in manufacturing industries. Kansas adds similar information concerning the miners and meatpackers.[1] Wisconsin presents a compilation of daily pay, distinguishing males and females; the other three states tabulate weekly wages and distinguish men, women, and children or young persons.[2] In each of these states, every important manufacturing industry is accorded separate presentation, and a summary is made for all industries. These reports undoubtedly contain the best wage statistics that are regularly made available in the United States to-day. In the first place, the classified presentation shows how earnings are distributed—averages alone could not do this. Second, continued use of a good method allows a study of the trend of wages from year to year. Third, an accurate comparison of the conditions of employment in the different groups of industry is made possible. Fourth, the figures are furnished regularly by manufacturers from their books, and should, therefore, be as exact as it is possible for statistics to be. Fifth, supplementary data regarding the state of employment, the proportion of business done in the industry, and the hours of labor are available, especially for Massachusetts and New Jersey. Sixth, the returns are complete, covering nearly every factory wage-worker in each of the states. With

[1] The 1911 Kansas report, the latest, omits these statistics. It is to be hoped that the omission is for one year only.

[2] In Kansas and New Jersey employees under sixteen years of age are reckoned children; in Massachusetts those under twenty-one are styled young persons.

all these merits there are some minor defects. First, except in the Wisconsin reports, the distribution is not given for the extremes, the groups being " under $3 " and " $25 and over ", and the classes are not uniform, running " $8 but under $9 ", " $9 but under $10 ", " $10 but under $12 ", " $12 but under $15 ", " $15 but under $20 ": this is a defect for some theoretic purposes, interpolation not being entirely satisfactory. Second, as the data refer to one week only, it is impossible to draw safe conclusions as to the annual earnings. Third, the practice of some bureaus of having each firm make returns for its " busy week ", the week of largest employment, makes it impossible to be sure that duplications are avoided; that is, the same individual may figure in the statistics from more than one concern: probably, however, no better week could be chosen as a sample, although a normal or typical week, as used by Wisconsin, might serve. Fourth, a suspicion has been expressed that the manufacturers are not always as careful as they might be to have the replies accurate, the filling of detailed questionnaires is expensive; there may be a difference between the possibility and the probability of securing exact figures from the books of the employer, if he does the compiling. Fifth, the average weekly earnings are not given except in Wisconsin. Taken all in all, however, the wage data furnished by these four commonwealths is unequaled in the United States for scope and method, and reliability.

The valuable data furnished in these reports for factory operatives are supplemented by the publications of New York. In the annual reports of the Bureau of Labor Statistics, appear what amount to the individual returns of the total earnings of the men and women trade-unionists during the first quarter and during the third quarter of the year. These are summarized by trade groups, and the earnings classified as being, for the three months, " less than

$75 ", " $75 to $149 ", " $150 to $224 ", " $225 and over ".
The raw material for this compilation is furnished by the
secretaries of the locals, and may, therefore, be more or
less inaccurate. New York's policy has been open to objection also on the ground that the figures cover only organized workers. In a way, these criticisms are both well
taken. Yet it cannot be denied that, in furnishing regularly
statistics of the earnings of union men and women, a unique
service is rendered; although it might be wished, perhaps,
that the earnings of unorganized workers were given in
parallel columns for the sake of comparison. But with
such excellent wage data for the employees of the manufacturers furnished by the neighboring states of New Jersey
and Massachusetts, it is surely an advantage to have New
York spend its energies in investigating the building trades,
public employment, theaters and music, and transportation.
Of course the conditions in no two states are exactly alike,
and yet, until larger appropriations are available, a division
of tasks seems wise. Finally, the adoption of three months
instead of the week as the unit of time seems to be a step in
advance; on the other hand, it would be well to have the
income group intervals in the summaries smaller, say
twenty-five instead of seventy-five dollars. On the whole,
then, New York's contribution is inferior to none.

Besides these five states which regularly present classified
statistics, there are a number which publish averages, sometimes minutely subdivided with regard to sex, industry, occupation, and locality. Chief among these commonwealths
is Ohio; but Pennsylvania, Michigan, Missouri, Washington,
and Tennessee compile some excellent figures of this class.
The other state bureaus, with occasional exceptions, print
no wage data worthy the name. With respect to salaries,
a few means are to be found in the Ohio, Michigan, and
Missouri reports, but the information is hardly in usable
form; and of contingent incomes, no figures are published.

Since but five states publish classified wage statistics, and only two have made any pretense of securing periodic data upon annual earnings, very little can be gained for a study of the Distribution of Incomes from these reports. Much that is valuable should be credited to these bureaus of labor, but, to say the least, they fail to throw a flood of light upon the important problem of this essay. Therefore, recourse must be had to federal sources. Among the publications of the Census, the Bureau of Labor, and the Department of Agriculture, there appears, at first blush, an enormous amount of pertinent data—not, to be sure, information dealing directly with incomes, but what are, nevertheless, desirable wage studies. In order to determine just what is available for the purpose of this essay, it will be well to subject these figures to closer scrutiny.

By all odds the best of the Census wage data are to be found in the study entitled *Employees and Wages,* a special volume published in 1903, and known, because it was prepared under the supervision of Professor Davis Rich Dewey, as the " Dewey Report ". For a large number of factory employees, male and female, above and below the sixteen-year line, the hourly and weekly wages are minutely classified. Separate presentations are accorded to the chief occupations of each of thirty-four leading manufacturing industries, the absolute numbers and the cumulative per cents in the several pay groups for 1890 and 1900 in identical establishments being set down in parallel columns. A further distinction is drawn between the different sections of the country. This report has many merits, among which may be mentioned: first, that the collection and the criticism of the data seems to have been more intelligently painstaking in this investigation than in any other; second, that the classification is so minute that many rearrangements are possible at the will of the student; third, that, as the occupational figures for 1890 and 1900 are published in parallel columns, it is possible to compare the wages paid by identical establishments for the two periods; fourth, that piece pay is put upon a time basis. Thus, the *Dewey Report* has the three prime virtues of a statistical publication, accuracy, detailed presentation, and a foundation for comparisons; yet, in certain respects, it might have been rendered more serviceable. First, there is no summary either for all the male factory employees, or for all those having the same occupation though employed in different industries, or for all those in one section of the country. Thus, the student being lost in a mass of detail, any general idea of the state of wages is impossible, as few persons have the ability, the facilities, and the time, to make their own summaries from such minute classifications. It was not until four years after the publication of the *Dewey Report* that Professor Moore made generally available a summary of its contents so far as they concerned adult males. Second, rates of pay are published, and, as has been pointed out, the whole effect of unemployment is necessarily neglected. This, however, is a disadvantage which attaches itself to nearly every wage study and will not be referred to again, although it should be kept constantly in mind. It might be wished that the scope of this investigation had been extended beyond the somewhat narrow field of manufactures, but the task would probably have been too great for one effort. At any rate, the *Dewey Report* is a model of most that is desirable in a work on wages.

In addition to this excellent *Dewey Report,* the Twelfth Census, in the volume on *Mines and Quarries,* offers statistics of the classified wages of the employees of " incorporated companies ". Separate presentations are given for each branch of mining in which a thousand or more wage-earners are employed, including anthracite and bituminous

coal, copper, lead, iron, gold, and silver, and for mines and
quarries as a whole. The value of these figures is impaired
by the following considerations: first, no occupational divisions are made, inside and outside workmen, for instance,
being included in the same tabulation; second, no distinction
is made for age, 11,857 boys being included among the total
of 581,728 employees; third, mining and quarrying as a
whole are not perfectly represented by the incorporated
companies; fourth, the demand for labor in mining coal is
notoriously irregular. On the other hand, the choice of the
classified method of presentation is a great step in advance
of most wage studies, and one should remember that this
investigation of earnings was but an incidental part of a
much larger study.

Never intended to reveal incomes, the Twefth Census,[1]
in the report on *Agriculture,* presents a tabulation of farms
by the " Value of Products of 1899 not fed to Live Stock."
This classification would be exactly what is needed to show
the distribution of incomes among farmers were it not that
two important allowances ought first to be made. A large proportion of farmers find it necessary to employ outside help,
and another group hire their lands. Obviously unless wages
and rent are first subtracted from the product, the amount
available to the agricultural family for actual enjoyment is
not disclosed. It may be asked why rent should be deducted
from the income of the farmer, and not from that of the
urbanite. The answer is that the rent paid by the agri-
culturalist is largely one of his costs of production; he hires
acres somewhat as others borrow capital; shelter for himself
and family is only one consideration. In spite of their short-
comings for this purpose, these tables may be used to show
with some precision the number of farm families whose in-

---

[1] Vol. v, *Agriculture,* pt. i, pp. lix *et seq.*

comes do not exceed a certain minimum. This use, however, is liable to one source of error which may be very important. In the case of some farmers, instead of a subtraction for rent and wages, an addition should be made for the return from a second place owned and let out; the number of such cases is unknown. The use of these tables in a study of the distribution of incomes, is, therefore, limited.

The schedules of the *Census of Manufactures,* taken in 1905 to cover the year 1904, called for classifications of the wages of men, women, and children under sixteen years of age. These returns were compiled in a table covering some 3,297,819 individual operatives of whom 2,619,053 were men.[1] Upon this basis, an estimate was made for the five and a half million wage-earners employed in all the manufacturing establishments of the United States. This estimate was derived with great care, the distribution of earnings in each industry being calculated separately for the average number of persons of each class employed in 1904; what was lacking in the *Dewey Report* was here supplied. The good features of this study may be mentioned: first, a broad base was used, forty-seven per cent of the factory wage-earners being included; second, not rates but *earnings* for the busy week were tabulated; third, the returns were prepared from actual records, verbal statements being accepted only in case there were less than ten employed in an establishment; fourth, the summary is excellently presented. Yet there are some things that might have been wished. In the first place, no details are given for those paid less than $3 per week, and such important groups as " $10 to $12 ", and " $12 to $15 " might better have been broken into classes with a one-dollar interval. This, however, is not a

[1] *Special Reports of the Census Office, Manufactures,* 1905, pt. iv, pp. 645 *et seq.*

vital point, particularly when one recalls the classification used in Massachusetts, New Jersey, and Kansas, and the fact that a more minute grouping would have made cumbrous the publication of the details by industries and by states. In the second place, there is a justifiable suspicion that the collection of the data was not as careful as might have been desired.[1] How much allowance should be made for carelessness of special agents is a question that cannot be answered. It would seem safe to assume that the estimates of proprietors would not minimize wages, and that a check was placed upon the size of errors by comparisons of the wage classification in each establishment with the amount of the weekly pay roll.[2] Finally, the marked similarity between the results of the Census of 1905 and the *Dewey Report* would seem to indicate approximate accuracy.[3]

In a special report upon *Central Electric Light and Power Plants*, 1902, the Census Bureau compiled the classified daily wages of the 18,878 employees in the most important occupations of about eighty per cent of the stations in the country. This seems to be the only other Census publication that thoroughly treats the subject of wages, although in the bulletins on the *Express Business, Telephones and Telegraphs, Street Railways,* and the *Shipping Industry,* many averages are presented.

There are, then, four recent reports of the Census office which are of service in a study of the distribution of in-

---

[1] "There is every reason to believe that at prior censuses the information in most cases was not taken from actual records, but was based on more or less inaccurate estimates of the operator of the factory." E. Dana Durand, *Quarterly Pub. American Statistical Association,* vol. xii, p. 65, March, 1910.

[2] *Census, Manufactures,* 1905, pt. iv, p. 644, a.

[3] *Infra,* p. 99.

comes; two of them deal with wages in manufactures, one with the pay of miners and quarrymen, and one with the receipts of farm families. Each of these investigations has certain defects for the purpose of this essay, and yet each, having also many excellencies, may furnish valuable material. The principal regret is that the field covered is so narrow, no effort having been made to study the wages of agricultural laborers, railway employees, and many other large groups of workingmen. A second sorrow is that the Thirteenth Census is to include no investigation of this important subject, and, consequently, in comparison with the new population and occupational figures now appearing, the available income statistics will seem even more ancient. It may be because the Census has done so much, that it seems to have left so much undone.

Satisfactory data not being found in the Census publications, it is natural to look elsewhere. As farming is such a fundamental branch of enterprise, and as labor forms so important a part of the cost of producing crops, it is reasonable to suppose that the Department of Agriculture would be able to furnish good wage statistics. And yet the search for adequate figures is vain. True, some nineteen or twenty studies have been made, but the total result is a collection of averages so general that they are almost devoid of meaning. Perhaps this use of the average may be justified: the employer wants to know what a hired man ought to cost him, and the average tells that well enough. Doubtless this is in a measure true, and yet, even from the viewpoint of the farmer it might be better to know the range and the distribution of wages; to know what must be paid for a good hand and what is the price of a poor one. But waving this as impracticable, the arithmetic mean has no significance to the agricultural laborer; it does not tell him what he can reasonably expect, nor how peculiar efficiency will be re-

warded. If the problem of securing farm labor is really as
acute as it is pictured, the figures which would allure men
into the field would be those showing classified annual earnings, and the chances for a hired man to rise to ownership—
provided these figures are attractive when compiled. Significant for this essay is the fact that there are no good statistics of the distribution of earnings among agricultural
workers.

Another federal organization that compiles wage statistics on a large scale is the Interstate Commerce Commission. In the *Statistics of the Railways,* there are regularly
tables showing separately for the ten geographic groups and
for the country as a whole, the average daily rates of pay
of the employees in each large occupational division—general officers, office clerks, station agents, and conductors, for
example. Highly probable it may be that in a given occupation remuneration is fairly uniform, nevertheless, it is
unsafe to accept, with Professor Nearing, these daily averages, as an indication of the distribution of annual incomes
among the labor force. Then, too, there are some women
among the employees of these carriers, but they are not dis-
tinguished in the tables. This, however, is not a matter of
great importance, since in 1900 only 1,688 of the 582,150
railway workers were females.[1] Members of the Interstate
Commerce Commission correctly believe that for inclusive-
ness and accuracy their wage data are unsurpassed.

Special documents submitted to Congress contain a great
deal of scattered and often unusable material relevant to the
subject of distribution of incomes. One of the most recent
of these, for instance, the Report of the Select Committee
on Wages and Prices of Commodities,[2] is little more than a

[1] *Abstract of the Twelfth Census,* p. 25.
[2] *Sen. Doc.* no. 847, 61st Cong., 3d Ses.

new edition of data already available in other federal publications. Although here and there the testimony of an individual brings out a few particular facts as to wages in some one branch of industry, these persons speak only from their own more or less limited experience, and their information cannot be considered sufficient for statistical use.

There remains for consideration the work of one other federal agency. Upon the Bureau of Labor naturally falls the duty of providing information relative to standards of living in the United States, and to the distribution of the means of maintaining those standards. *The Eighteenth Annual Report of the Commissioner of Labor* (1903), well conceived and skilfully executed, is the most extensive existing compendium of material upon these subjects. Although the title of this study was "The Cost of Living", the subject was treated so broadly as to make it useful in many different lines of research. Special agents visited at random working-class families. An attempt was made to distribute these households among the various industries approximately in proportion to their importance, and among the commonwealths according to population; thus the final result may be considered fairly typical of the whole United States. It was further intended to deal only with families having a total income not over $1,200. Both these aims seem to have been fairly achieved. The agents secured answers to quite an elaborate set of questions, calculated to show the amount and the composition of the income, the details of its expenditure, and the membership of the households. In all, 25,440 schedules were returned. The wages for the year of the 24,402 male heads of families were classified, by occupations and by industries, in one-hundred-dollar groups, and thus were made to afford an excellent presentation of the distribution of annual earnings among mature men in the industrial pursuits. There are many reasons for commending this report. First, the information was gathered by trained special agents, and an endeavor was made to secure consistency in each return by various checking expedients.[1] Second, classification is undoubtedly the best arrangement of data on incomes, earnings, and unemployment. Third, annual compensations, not wage rates, are tabulated. Fourth, the remuneration of heads of families is presented; it is an important question whether the mature man is able by his own exertion to support a home. Fifth, great effort was made to have the result typical of the entire industrial people of the United States. Sixth, the base is the broadest in all the American studies of household budgets and revenues. From the standpoint of the student of Social Science, this *Eighteenth Annual Report of the Commissioner of Labor* is certainly the best index of the possibilities of the American workingman for self realization. As a treatment of the distribution of incomes, however, it leaves something to be desired. In the first place, the schedules apply to the years 1900, 1901, and 1902, and consequently, it is questionable whether in this rapidly-developing country, the conclusions as to the distribution of earnings are still valid. In the second place, although many occupations were represented among the twenty-four thousand men, only fifty-seven trades contributed as many as a hundred schedules each. Moreover, as the investigation was confined largely to families having incomes not over $1,200, the tables cannot show the exact state of affairs except in those occupations where the absolute high limit of earnings is $1,200 or less. These two facts considerably narrow the usefulness of this report. Finally, the nomenclature of occupations is not identical with that of the Census. In spite of these limitations, the results of this investigation may prove to be of great value.

---

[1] For details, consult the opening pages of the report itself.

Studies, similar in general scope to that just discussed, have been made in the cotton, woolen, and glass industries, but they are too old for use to-day. In the bi-monthly *Bulletins of the Bureau of Labor* there are many articles on wages, but none of any importance presents classified data. Until 1907, an index number of wages was annually published. Although some criticism might be passed upon the method of computing this index, it had the merit of taking into consideration the rates of pay in the building trades as well as in manufactures. Two recent special studies of the Bureau of Labor deserve mention, the *Report on the Strike at the Bethlehem Steel Works,* and the *Investigation of Telephone Companies.*[1] The former presents classified hourly, and the latter monthly earnings. But these are both very special for the purposes of this essay. The latest work of the Bureau is the *Report on Condition of Woman and Child Wage-Earners in the United States,*[2] in nineteen volumes. The method of arranging the data in this report is admirable, and the material has undoubtedly been collected with great care. The figures of earnings, however, relate almost exclusively to women, or children, or to men in occupations where women and children are normally employed, and are therefore of little value to this study.

This survey of the sources of information seems clearly to indicate that material for a convincing study of the distribution of incomes in the United States, does not exist. In this field, the Iowa and Kansas returns from individual workingmen being at once haphazard and too narrow in scope, the states have no regularly-organized statistics. Four commonwealths, however, Massachusetts, New Jersey, Kansas, and Wisconsin, periodically publish tables classify-

[1] *Sen. Doc.* nos. 521 and 380, 61st Cong., 2d Ses.
Sen. Doc. no. 645, 61st Cong., 2d Ses.

ing the pay of factory operatives; and New York renders similar service for the quarterly earnings of organized workers. Only these five states furnish information in any way satisfactory for the purpose in hand. Nor does the Federal Government fully meet the need. The *Dewey Report* and the 1905 *Census of Manufactures* offer a mass of excellent wage data for the one branch of industry; the volumes on *Mines and Quarries,* and on *Agriculture* afford valuable hints; the *Eighteenth Annual Report of the Commissioner of Labor* furnishes a real tabulation of the distribution of earnings in certain occupations; special studies, excellent in their fields, are diverse in method, and rarely throw light on the problem. Thus is the conclusion enforced that a plain statement of the distribution of labor incomes in the United States is impossible.

So much for the statistics of labor earnings; even less satisfactory is the material for a study of other forms of income. In the Census is recorded the number of families, urban and rural, owning their dwellings; the value of this real estate is approximately known; but, as was pointed out in Chapter III, even in the case of farms, the number of owners cannot be ascertained from any published data, much less their returns from property. So far as they go, the accuracy and the value of the Census figures are not here questioned, but they are simply insufficient to show the distribution of real property in the United States.

Many valuable special investigations have been made by the Census Bureau, for instance, that of 1880 into the ownership of United States bonds, the summary of which was presented in Chapter III, and that of 1904 into the debts of the states and minor civil divisions.[1] Other reports have been prepared on the *Street Railways,* the *Tele-*

---

[1] *Census—Wealth, Debt and Taxation,* 1904.

phone Companies, the *Telegraph Companies, Central Electric Light and Power Stations,* and *Mines and Quarries.* All of these show the stock and bond capitalization, the interest, and the dividends, but they are inadequate for the present study, in that they give no idea of the number of stock and bond holders. In the *Census of Manufactures* it is customary to print a warning against trying to determine net gain from the published figures, which are collected with the distinct understanding that profits are not to be revealed. There was, however, one departure from this policy when, in 1900, the dividends of each of the 185 " Industrial Combinations " were published, but in this case no computation was made of the interest on the funded debt. It is, therefore, apparent that little aid can be expected from the Census publications.

The Interstate Commerce Commission annually compiles the book, already mentioned, entitled, *Statistics of the Railways.* This volume includes excellent material on the earnings of both stocks and bonds, classifying the stocks according to the rate of dividend. The last two years have seen the beginning of a new publication by this Commission, the *Report on Express Companies,* which contains complete information as to the capitalization and earnings of these enterprises. But since the special computation of the number of stockholders in 1904, nothing has been done to show the public the number of persons owning railway or express securities.

Accurate figures of the capitalization and earnings of all classes of banks are published in the annual reports of the Comptroller of Currency. The new special excise tax on corporations has occasioned the introduction into the reports of the Secretary of the Treasury of a table showing the capitalization and net income of all the incorporated companies in the United States.

For the data as to the capitalization and earnings of individual corporations, recourse must be had to private publications, such as the stock exchange manuals, and the financial journals.

The information in all of these publications has but one fault for the purpose of this study; the matter of ownership is not treated. There is no basis for the determination either of the number of recipients of property incomes, or of the distribution of these incomes according to size.

This completes the survey of the sources of material for a study of the distribution of incomes in the United States. It remains to point out what inferences have been drawn from the available data, what inferences are permissible, and what steps are necessary in order to secure adequate statistics.

CHAPTER V

PREVIOUS TREATMENT OF AMERICAN INCOME STATISTICS

THE first elaborate study of the distribution of incomes in the United States was based upon very special sources. Although it is true that Dr. Charles B. Spahr both availed himself of official figures showing the distribution among individuals of taxable property in the rural portion of Massachusetts in 1873 and quoted from the 1890 Census returns of home ownership, his really constructive work was founded entirely upon an original compilation of the probate statistics of New York. Estates worth as much as $5,000 were subject to an inheritance tax. It appeared that almost exactly one-eighth of the men who died after passing the twenty-fifth birthday, left such estates, and that the number of males over twenty-five years of age was practically identical with the number of private families. Consequently, the distribution of estates among dying men should be typical of the distribution of property among households. With this preface, the conclusions may be outlined in Dr. Spahr's own words:

The distribution of wealth in the whole state of New York is of less importance than the distribution in the district lying outside of the two great cities. This district is typical of the country at large; for if the distribution of property is wider in the distinctively agricultural states, it is much narrower in the excluded Metropolis. The table for the state at large, outside of New York and Brooklyn ran as follows: [1]

[1] *The Present Distribution of Wealth in the United States*, p. 64. Spahr's records covered thirty-six of the sixty-one counties.

TABLE V

DISTRIBUTION OF ESTATES IN NEW YORK

I.	II.	III.	IV.	V.
Value of estates.	Number.	Realty.	Personalty.	Total.
$50,000 or over...............	36	$2,188,540	$6,606,123	$8,794,663
5,000 to $50,000	409	2,950,325	2,233,871	5,184,196
Under $5,000	1,427	989,668	1,095,430	2,085,098
	1,872	$6,128,533	$9,935,424	$16,063,957

The table for New York City showed that one-eighth of all the families held more than $5,000 worth of property. The census investigation of mortgages showed that about one-eighth of the farms of the country were worth more than $5,000. With a normal death rate the table for New York outside the two great cities shows just the same proportion of well-to-do families. We may therefore say with much precision, that approximately one-eighth of the families of the nation, city, town, and country hold more than $5,000. The proportion holding over $50,000 is exceptionally great in the large cities, and exceptionally small in the country districts; but the proportion in the intermediate territory selected may be safely assumed for the entire nation. The table for the nation at large would therefore read: [1]

TABLE VI

SPAHR'S ESTIMATE OF DISTRIBUTION OF PROPERTY IN THE UNITED STATES

I.	II.	III.
Property group.	Number of families.	Aggregate wealth.
$50,000 and over	125,000	$33,000,000,000
50,000 to $5,000..................	1,375,000	23,000,000,000
Under $5,000	11,000,000	9,000,000,000
	12,500,000	$65,000,000,000

[1] *The Present Distribution of Wealth in the United States*, p. 66.

To sum up the reasoning so far: there are in the United States 12,500,000 private families. Of these one-eighth, 1,500,000 (1,562,500), own not less than $5,000 worth of property each; $\frac{36}{409 + 36}$ or $\frac{36}{445}$ of these 1,500,000, or 125,000 (121,348) families are possessed of at least $50,000. The average wealth of the thirty-six families is about $264,000 ($8,794,663 ÷ 36 = $244,295), therefore, their total wealth is $264,000 × 125,000 or $33,000,000,000. Similarly $23,000,000,000 is obtained as the total wealth of the 1,375,000 families worth from $5,000 to $50,000. The $9,-000,000,000 seems to be obtained by subtracting $56,000,-000,000 from $65,000,000,000.[1]

From the distribution of property, it is but a step to the distribution of incomes. " Nearly every family possessing $50,000 worth of property receives an aggregate family income of $5,000. Likewise, most families possessing over $5,000 receive an aggregate income exceeding $1,200 . . . exceptions are practically offset by the families who receive the income specified without possessing the specified amount of property." Since, however, six per cent of Boston families then dwelt in houses the rental value of which would indicate an income not under $5,000, and since in New York City there were " as many families with $5,000 incomes as with $30,000 property," it was concluded that about two hundred thousand households enjoyed such incomes. The incomes of the families worth less than $5,000 are almost entirely from labor, and are reckoned as less than $1,200. Thus, with some observations as to the averages, it is concluded that the distribution of incomes in the United States is as follows:

[1] See *Census, Wealth Debt, and Taxation*, 1904, p. 29.

TABLE VII

SPAHR'S ESTIMATE OF DISTRIBUTION OF INCOMES IN THE UNITED STATES[1]

I.	II.	III.	IV.	V.	VI.
	Number of families.	Average income from labor.	Aggregate income.		
Family income.			From labor.	From capital.	Total.
$5,000 and over	200,000	$3,500	$700,000,000	$2,410,000,000	$3,110,000,000
$5,000 to $1,200	1,300,000	1,200	1,560,000,000	1,330,000,000	2,890,000,000
Under $1,200..	11,000,000	380	4,200,000,000	600,000,000	4,800,000,000
	12,500,000	$517 [2]	$6,460,000,000	$4,340,000,000	$10,800,000,000

These estimates of Dr. Spahr have been so widely quoted that they must be accorded some attention. In this brief compass it is impossible to do full justice to his argument, but surely the foregoing bald summary does not materially misrepresent his reasoning. Dr. Spahr's conclusion rests upon the assumption that, so far as the distribution of wealth is concerned, thirty-six counties in New York State are typical of the entire Union. The facts, if ever observed, may justify this premise, but they may not. Moreover, the postulate that the revenues of households worth less than $5,000 never exceed $1,200, that the ownership of $5,000 worth of property indicates an income of over $1,200, and that possessions aggregating $50,000 insure the opportunity of annually expending at least $5,000, may be a very shrewd surmise, but is none the less a guess based upon the experience of one man. Resting thus on two rather questionable assumptions, the estimate of Dr. Spahr is not as satisfactory as it might be.[3]

[1] Spahr, *op. cit.*, p. 128.

[2] Not in Spahr's table.

[3] Every estimate involves assumptions, but some assumptions are much more venturesome than others. Both of Dr. Spahr's assumptions are rather bold.

In the reasoning of Dr. Spahr, there are other points worthy of attention. For instance, it is not clear whether the estates of women are included in the tabulations, or whether any allowance should be made for property held in the wife's name. Again, it is probable that many farms are passed from father to son as gifts or sales, transfers which would not be recorded in probate returns.[1] Professor Mayo-Smith raised the point that no account was taken of the ages of those who left estates: it may very well be true that many young men who died without wealth, were on the road to acquisition, and would have accumulated considerable property had they lived longer. Thus the argument tends to over-emphasize the concentration of wealth. Finally, Dr. Spahr's trust in " common observation " may not be quite justified, for it is so extremely easy to see " what is behind one's eyes." [2]

It appears, then, that Dr. Spahr's conclusions cannot be accepted as a satisfactory description of the distribution of incomes. The estimate may be a close approximation to the facts, but the method is open to so many valid criticisms that without confirmation the results are inconclusive. With a larger base, perhaps, such as the French returns on " Successions and Donations " or the statistics of the English " Death Duties ", analogous processes might be used to advantage in discussing the ownership of property, but even this data would hardly be a sound foundation for an estimate of the distribution of incomes.

---

[1] *Census*, 1900, vol. v, *Agriculture*, pt. i, pp. lxxx, lxxxix, col. 2.

[2] " The writer has learned, and hopes to teach, that, upon matters coming within its field, the common observation of common people is more trustworthy than the statistical investigations of the most unprejudiced experts. Indeed, he has come to believe that social statistics are only trustworthy when they show to the world at large what common observation shows to those personally familiar with the conditions described." Spahr, *op. cit.*, preface.

Another attempt to formulate a general description of the distribution of compensation in the United States was made in 1911, but the study was confined almost exclusively to an investigation of the earnings of factory operatives and railway employees. In his primary task of calling attention to the inadequacy of American wage statistics, Professor Nearing [1] has been eminently successful, but in his method of attack, in utilizing the available material, he is not quite so fortunate. His argument may be briefly illustrated.

The classified wages of men in the factories of Massachusetts are presented in the following table.

TABLE VIII

CLASSIFIED WAGES, MALES TWENTY-ONE YEARS AND OVER, MASSACHUSETTS, 1908 [2]

I.	II.	III.	IV.
Classified weekly earnings.	Males 21 years and over.	Per cent.	Cumulative [3] per cent.
Under $5	5,049	1	1
$5 to 6	6,216	2	3
6 to 7	13,584	4	7
7 to 8	22,469	7	14
8 to 9	31,472	9	23
9 to 10	41,399	12	35
10 to 12	61,632	17	52
12 to 15	70,293	20	72
15 to 20	69,996	20	92
20 and over...........	28,008	8	100
Totals	350,118	100	

These wage rates, however, taken by themselves, are by

[1] *Wages in the United States*, 1908-1910.

[2] *Wages in the United States*, p. 43; or *23d Ann. Rep't. Statistics of Manufactures*, Mass., p. 82.

[3] Cumulative per cents not given by Nearing.

no means representative of annual earnings,[1] for allowances must be made for unemployment. The factories of the state reported 275 days worked out of 305 business days; in other words, these concerns were idle twelve per cent of the working time. Therefore, "the table of Classified Weekly Earnings, after being multiplied by 52, must be reduced by 12 per cent, in order to represent an accurate average for the year. The stated weekly earnings, after subtracting 12 per cent for unemployment, would give, in annual earnings, the percentages" in the following table:

TABLE IX

CUMULATIVE PERCENTAGES OF ADULT MALES RECEIVING CLASSIFIED YEARLY EARNINGS (UNEMPLOYMENT DEDUCTED), ALL MASSACHUSETTS INDUSTRIES, 1908 [2]

Classified yearly earnings.	Adult males, per cent.	Classified yearly earnings.	Adult males, per cent.
Under $229........	1	Under $459	35
" 275.........	2	" 549	52
" 320.........	5	" 686	72
" 366........	12	" 915	92
" 412........	21	Over 915	8

After corresponding tables have been presented for the four leading industries of the state the conclusion is reached

that not more than one adult male wage-earner in every twenty employed in the industries of Massachusetts receives, in annual earnings, for a normally prosperous year, more than $1,000. On the other hand, more than one-third of all the adult males are paid wages under $500; more than one-half receive wages under $600; while nearly three-quarters receive less than $700 annually.[3]

[1] Nearing, *op. cit.*, pp. 49, 51, 52.
[2] *Ibid.*, p. 51, table on p. 52. Compare Table VIII, column iv.
[3] *Ibid.*, p. 57.

Tables, similarly altered, are drawn from the New Jersey
and Kansas reports, the results showing a marked harmony.
Additional certainty is given to the deductions by figures
quoted from the special reports of the Bureau of Labor on
the *Strike at the Bethlehem Steel Works,* and the *Telephone
Companies.*

An exceedingly novel method is introduced in dealing
with the wages of railway employees. The second, third,
and fourth columns of the following table are taken from
the *Statistics of the Railways,*[1] the first and fifth being supplied by Professor Nearing.

From this table it is concluded that " in 1909, 51 per cent
of the million and a half railroad employees of the United
States received less than $625 per year;[2] that 93 per cent
received less than $1,000 per year, leaving 7 per cent who
earned more than $1,000 annually."

[1] 1909, pp. 34, 40.
[2] Nearing, *op. cit.*, p. 176.

TABLE X

DISTRIBUTION OF WAGES IN THE VARIOUS EMPLOYMENTS. RAILROADS OF THE
UNITED STATES, 1909 [1]

I.	II.	III.	IV.	V.
Average daily wages.		Number.	Average daily wages.	Per cent.
Over $10....	General officers	5,492	$12.67	
$5 to 10....	Other officers	8.022	6.40	
4 to 5 ...	Enginemen	57,077	4.44	4
3 to 4....	Conductors	43,608	3.81	3
2 to 3....	Machinists	48,237	2.98	
	Firemen	60,349	2.67	
	Other trainmen..............	114,760	2.59	
	Carpenters	60,867	2.43	
	Employees—account floating equipment................	8,758	2.31	
	General office clerks	69,959	2.31	
	Telegraph operators and dispatchers..................	39,115	2.30	
	Other shopmen	195,110	2.13	
	Station agents	36,519	2.08	
	Total $2 to $3	633,674		42
1 to 2	All other employees and laborers	210,898	1.98	
	Section foremen	41,859	1.96	
	Other station men	136,733	1.82	
	Switch tenders, crossing tenders and watchmen	44,608	1.73	
	Other trackmen	320,762	1.38	
	Total $1 to $2	754,950		51
	Total employees	1,502,823		100

The most important of the tables presented by Professor
Nearing are brought together for comparison in the last
chapter of his book as follows:

[1] Nearing, *op. cit.*, p. 175.

TABLE XI

CUMULATIVE PERCENTAGES OF MALES RECEIVING CERTAIN CLASSIFIED WEEKLY
EARNINGS, COMPILED FROM CERTAIN REPORTS, 1908–1910 [1]

I.	II.	III.	IV.	V.	VI.	VII.	VIII.
Classified weekly earnings.	Massachusetts, 1908 (21 years and over).	New Jersey, 1909 (16 years and over).	Kansas, 1909 (16 years and over).	Wisconsin, 1906–7 (all males).	Bell Telephone Company, 1910 (all males).	Bethlehem Steel Works, 1910 (all males).	Railroads of the United States, 1909 (all males).
Under $8	12	18	8	12	5	8	22
Under $12..................	52	57	46	59	23	60	51
Under $15...........	72	74	70	89	32	75	78
Under $20..................	92	91	91	98	80	92	92
$20 and over	8	9	9	2	20	8	8
Total employed	350,118	204,782	50,720	128,334	171,139	9,184	1,502,823

But in proceeding to annual earnings some allowance must be made for unemployment. This is done by the following reasoning: approximately " one-half of the adult males working in the industrial sections of the United States " are employed at a rate not over $12 per week, or $600 per year.

Three-quarters are paid less than $750 annually and less than one-tenth earn $1,000 a year. . . . These figures are not accurate, however, since they are all gross figures, including unemployment. They should be reduced by, perhaps, 20 per cent, varying with the year, the location and the industry. There may be no general agreement as to what reduction should be made,—but some reduction is obviously necessary. Making, therefore, a reduction of one-fifth, it appears that half of the

---

[1] Nearing, *op. cit.*, p. 210. The total at the foot of column vi should be 15,326. *Investigation of Telephone Companies*, p. 294. A similar summary is made for the wages of women.

adult males of the United States are earning less than $500 a year; that three-quarters of them are earning less than $600 annually; that nine-tenths are receiving less than $800 a year; while less than ten per cent receive more than that figure.

This proportion applies to the United States " east of the Rockies and north of the Mason and Dixon Line ".[1]

These interesting conclusions of Professor Nearing have received so much publicity that it is necessary to consider the method by which they were reached. In the first place, although all the data, which serve as a base for the final estimate of annual wages of males, relate to the limited field of manufactures, railroading, and telephoning, the natural inference of the reader is that the conclusions apply to " the annual earnings of adult males (and females) employed east of the Rockies and north of the Mason and Dixon Line." In just what sense this inference is altered by the earlier allusion to " the industrial sections of the United States " can hardly be determined. Does the estimate, for instance, include all men employed at all tasks in urban communities, or only those who are engaged in what are generally known as " industrial pursuits "—manufactures, trade and transportation? Doubtless the latter is the correct interpretation, but it might advantageously be indicated more clearly in Professor Nearing's closing section.

It is the deduction of a certain per cent for unemployment.

---

[1] Nearing, op. cit., pp. 213, 214. Perhaps it would be only just to add Professor Nearing's closing words: " It is not important that the reported wages be reduced by one-fifth. The available unemployment data indicates that such a reduction is an approximately correct one; if, however, later studies show this estimate of unemployment to be excessive or inadequate, a corresponding alteration will be made in the summary of wages, but until such a study appears, the answer to the question, ' What are wages?' is contained in the above summary." The summary in Professor Nearing's book includes parallel deductions concerning the wages of adult females.

however, that particularly challenges attention. This process has been explained at length in connection with the general figures for Massachusetts, and later summarized in Professor Nearing's own words. Nine-tenths of the adult male factory operatives are employed at wage rates less than $20 per week; the average idleness is one-fifth of the working time; therefore, ninety per cent of these operatives earn less than $800 per annum. Such reasoning entirely disregards the actual distribution of unemployment. About half of the workers are unemployed for a week or more during the course of a normal year; of this half probably forty per cent are out of work at least ten weeks; thus approximately a fifth of the American factory or industrial people are idle as much as one-fifth of their time. This is not a dogmatic statement but is probably not far from the truth.[1] It is then preposterous to argue that, since the maximum earning power of nine-tenths of the adult males engaged in manufacturing is $1,040, and since the average loss of working time is twenty per cent, all these ninety per cent earn less than $800 ($832). Possibly some of these men worked continuously, perhaps a half did not lose more than two weeks or at most a month. Nearly sixty per cent of the 24,402 heads of families studied by the Bureau of Labor in 1901 were idle less than two weeks if at all; 1,660 of the 2,556 female department store employees investigated in Illinois in 1908, it will be remembered, figured in fifty weekly pay rolls; 32 blacking factories in Massachusetts were busy in 1908 an average of 305.22 days, six billiard table works, 306.33 days; six cotton-waste companies, 301.95 days; nine engraving and die-sinking establishments, 304.67 days, and, by way of contrast, 49 brick and tile con-

---

[1] See the *Eighteenth Annual Report of the Commissioner of Labor,* pp. 288, 289; also *Twelfth Census of the United States, 1900, Special Report on Occupations,* pp. ccxxvi-ccxxxv.

cerns averaged but 148.46 busy days.[1] The burden of unemployment is, therefore, very unevenly distributed among
industries and among individuals, and cannot be dealt with
by a simple reduction of maximum earnings. Doubtless
some of those men employed at $20 per week earned less
than $800 in the course of the year, but it is inconceivable
that *all* of them were idle *twelve weeks*. What the fraction
was, none can say. Not to quarrel, then, with Professor
Nearing's belief that twenty per cent of industrial working
time is lost, his method of deducting for unemployment is
misleading.

Another question of method arises in connection with
the treatment of the earnings of railroad employees. For
instance, in Professor Nearing's table, switch-tenders, crossing-tenders, and watchmen to the number of 44,698 are included in one group with average per diem wages of $1.73.
All these men, he reasons, receive daily between one and two
dollars, and, therefore, earn not more than $600, or, allow-
ing for unemployment, $500 per year. Now as a matter of
fact, of the 120 switchmen who were listed in the Bureau
of Labor investigation in 1901, sixty per cent earned more
than $600 and thirty-five per cent more than $700. Again,
the author lists all firemen as having labor incomes less than
$1,000, yet the official study showed seven per cent of these
men receiving more than that sum. Similarly, nearly forty
per cent of the engineers, whom Professor Nearing classes
as enjoying incomes over $1,000, actually received less.[2]
These concrete illustrations demonstrate better than argument the fallacy of maintaining that, if the average wages

[1] There were 307 business days in 1908. *Mass. Statistics of Manufactures,* 1908, pp. 121 *et seq.; Eighteenth Annual Report of the Commissioner of Labor,* p. 288; *Biennial Report, Bureau of Labor Statistics, Illinois,* 1908, pp. 426, 445.

[2] *Eighteenth Annual Report of the Commissioner of Labor,* p. 283.

of a given group of men is a certain amount, each individual in that category earns less than, or more than, some other specified sum. There appears no reason for assuming that the errors thus committed are counterbalancing, and, therefore, conclusions thus derived fail to carry conviction.

These two flaws in the method make it impossible to accept Professor Nearing's answer to the question, " What are Wages? " On the other hand, these adverse criticisms of his work serve but to confirm his main contention—that the development of wage statistics in the United States is extremely unsatisfactory.

Having thus briefly considered the two studies of distribution of incomes and of earnings in the United States which have a claim to scientific accuracy, it is well worth while to compare their conclusions with the results of European statistical compilations. For the year 1892, Dr. Spahr found that eighty-eight per cent of the twelve and a half million American families had incomes of $1,200 or less. According to Professor Nearing, in the years about 1908-1910, nine-tenths of the adult males engaged in industry east of the Rocky Mountains and north of the Mason and Dixon Line earned annually no more than $800, and the same proportion of women received in wages less than $500. Suppose that, in this group, the highest paid men marry the best remunerated women; even then, the annual earning power of ninety per cent of the couples dependent on industry would be under $1,300. Of course this supposition is purely fanciful; it disregards the contributions of children, and the possible intermarriages between men and women on different wage levels; but it seems to be the only way of comparing the results of the two American studies. In fact the conclusions are not parallel, for Spahr treated incomes of families in the United States as a whole, while Nearing devoted his attention to the earnings of individuals in a limited number of occupations in a definite fraction of the country.

On the other hand, there is a surprising coincidence between the figures of Dr. Spahr, and the conclusions of Professor Paul Leroy-Beaulieu. Basing his calculations upon the rentals of lodgings in Paris, the learned French economist found that, in 1896, probably 89.02 per cent of the families in that city were living on less than 7,000 francs ($1,351) a year and 1.86 per cent enjoyed incomes of not less than 32,000 francs ($6,176). These results are remarkably similar to those of Dr. Spahr, who estimated eighty-eight per cent of American families as having, in 1892, revenues less than $1,200, and one and six-tenths per cent over $5,000. As Professor Leroy-Beaulieu remarks, the proportion of high incomes is probably larger in Paris than in France as a whole; France, moreover, with the exception of Australia and the United Kingdom, is probably the richest country in the world.[1] The conclusions, therefore, are in a strict sense incomparable one applying to a great city, the other to a nation, yet the similarity is worth noting.[2]

In this connection the Prussian fiscal returns are also interesting. In 1905, for instance, out of a total population of over thirty-six million, 1,881,491 were entirely exempt from the assessment, and 20,483,263, or 56.48 per cent of the individual inhabitants, were attached to families no member of which enjoyed an income of 900 marks ($214.-20). Over ninety per cent of all the residents belonged to

---

[1] *Census, Wealth, Debt, and Taxation*, 1904, p. 35.

[2] Incomes were found by multiplying by ten rents over 7,000 fr.; by eight rents from 2,500 fr. to 6,999 fr.; by seven rents below 2,500 fr. Paul Leroy-Beaulieu, *Essai sur la répartition des richesses*, fourth edition, 1896, p. 563.

families no member of which had an income of 3,000 marks ($714). Suppose that each of the households in the class first mentioned had three members gainfully employed at the maximum of tax exemption (899 M.), there would still be approximately fifty-six per cent of the families in Prussia living on less than 2,700 M. ($643) per year. Is this supposition impossible? Are there many families in Prussia with four, five, and more providers? Possibly; yet for an industrial family in the United States to have a total revenue double that of its largest wage-earner is quite unusual, and a working-class household enjoying an income three times the compensation of its main supporter is a rarity indeed. In view of these considerations, and of the facts shown in Table XII, it is entirely safe to conclude that more than half, probably more than six-tenths, of the

Note 2, p. 80, continued:

RENTS AND INCOMES IN PARIS, JANUARY I, 1896

I.	II.	III.	
Classified rents.	Corresponding incomes.	Incomes.	
		Number.	Per cent.
Above 20,000 fr.	200,000 fr. or above.	495	.06
15,000–19,999 fr.	150,000 to 199,900 fr.	503	.06
10,000-14,999 fr.	100,000 to 149,900 fr.	1,572	.19
7,000– 9,999 fr.	56,000 to 99,900 fr.	2,954	.36
4,000– 6,999 fr.	32,000 to 55,900 fr.	9,757	1.19
2,500– 3,999 fr.	17,500 to 31,900 fr.	14,421	1.77
1,500– 2,499 fr.	10,500 to 17,400 fr.	26,526	3.25
1,000– 1,499 fr.	7,000 to 10,490 fr.	33,495	4.10
500– 999 fr.	3,500 to 6,990 fr.	117,695	14.42
300– 499 fr.	2,100 to 3,490 fr.	210,683	25.73
200– 299 fr.	1,400 to 2,090 fr.	199,440	24.44
Below 200 fr.	Below 1,400 fr.	198,599	24.43
Totals	....	816,140	100.00

TABLE XII

INCOME TAXES—PRUSSIA, 1905 [1]

Class of incomes.	Taxpayers.	Members of families.	Per cent of	
			Tax-payers.	Members of families.
Assessment remitted	....	1,881,491	......	5.19
Income under 900 M ($214.20)....	(not taxed on income) ..	20,483,263	......	56.48
M M				
900– 3,000 ($214–$714).......	3,889,171	12,262,036	88.58	33.81
3,000– 6,000 ($714–$1,428)	326,921	1,083,802	7.44	2.99
6,000– 9,500 ($1.428–$2,261)....	86,340	277,123	1.96	.76
9,500– 30,500 ($2,261–$7,259)....	70,943	227,251	1.62	.63
30,500–100,000 ($7,259–$23,800)...	14,374	45,454	.33	.12
Over 100,000 M (over $23,800)	2,859	9,019	.07	.02
Totals	4,390,608	34,387,948	100.00	100.00
Total including those whose assessment is remitted	....	36,269,439		

families of Prussia do not enjoy annual incomes of 2,700 M. ($643). That eighty-eight per cent of the persons who actually pay the income tax in Prussia should be assessed on no more than 3,000 M. ($714), indicates that wages in Germany must be lower than those of the industrial workingmen of the United States of whom ninety per cent, according to Professor Nearing earn less than $800 per annum. In discussing these French and German statistics, it must not be forgotten that prices vary from country to country. Even were the comparative costs of living known, a true contrast between the welfare of the inhabitants of different states could not be made without taking account of

[1] *Jahrbücher für National Oekonomie und Statistik, Volkswirtschaftliche Chronik*, 1906, vol. 87, pp. 489, 491.

the psychological differences of their people. The question of national well-being is extremely complicated.

Because of the separate assessment of (A) returns from the ownership of lands and houses, (B) revenues from the occupation of land, (C) annuities, dividends, and interest payable in the United Kingdom on government securities, (D) annual profits arising to persons residing in the United Kingdom from any kind of property wheresoever situated, or from any profession, trade, employment, or vocation wheresoever carried on; on annual profits arising to persons not resident in the United Kingdom from property wheresoever situated, or from any profession, trade, employment, or vocation exercised in the United Kingdom; and on interest of money, annuities, and other annual profits and gains, and (E) on incomes derived from public offices, or employments of profit, and on annuities, pensions, or stipends payable by her majesty, or out of the public revenue of the United Kingdom:—because personal receipts falling in these different schedules have been separately assessed, the British income tax supplies no answer to the question as to the distribution of incomes.[1] Schedules D and E include what the English know as " business and professional " incomes. In the fiscal year 1906-1907, there were 904,888 assessments of individuals in these two classes. The population of the Kingdom was about forty-four million, or, roughly, nine million families. Can it then be held that about one-tenth of the British households enjoy incomes of £160 or more? The answer depends on (1) the number of individuals figuring in both schedules D and E, (2) the number of persons assessed in the first three classes but not in the last two, (3) the number of persons enjoying revenues from several sources, aggregating over £160 but each

---

[1] Adams, *Finance,* p. 477.

less than that sum, and (4) the extent of evasions. There is also, now, a " Super-Tax " on incomes in excess of £5,000. Up to March 31, 1911, 10,287 such incomes were reported, and more returns were being received. The Commissioners of Inland Revenue would hazard nothing more than that there were over 10,600 individuals enjoying incomes of at least £5,000.[1] It is, therefore, unsafe to speculate upon the interpretation of these British income-tax returns.

TABLE XIII

INCOME TAX—UNITED KINGDOM, 1909–10[2]

(Part of Returns of Schedules D and E. The numbers are those of " Assessments," not of Taxpayers)

I.	II.	III.	IV.	V.	VI.
Income	Persons—not employees.	Local authorities.	Employees, D.	Employees, E.	Totals, persons.
Not exceeding £160 but not exempt..........	187,774	7,538	18,650	186,212	400,174
Exceeding £160 and not exceeding £200..	96,022	404	37,629	100,264	234,319
" 200 " " 500..	110,643	1,224	49,776	172,247	333,890
" 500 " " 1,000..	20,956	673	4,014	28,540	54,183
" 1,000 " " 5,000..	10,138	1,116	753	7,301	19,308
" £5,000	805	615	3	167	1,590
Totals	426,338	11,570	110,825	494,731	1,043,464

[1] *Report of the Commissioners of His Majesty's Inland Revenue for the year ended 31st March, 1911*, p. 99.

[2] *Fifty-fourth Report of the Commissioners of Inland Revenue for the year ended 31st March, 1911*, p. 132. The Royal Statistical Society conducted an investigation in 1910 to determine the distributions of incomes under £160 in the salaried classes. The numbers earning above

More significant, perhaps, for the present purpose, than the income tax, is the tax on the rental value of inhabited houses.

This table shows that about eighty per cent of the families of England and Scotland live in houses of an annual rental value under £20 or $97.33. Just what are the ratios of rents to incomes in Great Britain, is doubtful, but the recent report of the British Board of Trade showed that money wages in the United States are to money wages in England and Wales as 230 is to 100, and that rents in American cities are to rents in England and Wales as 207 is to 100. The fraction of the Englishman's income which goes for housing, therefore, cannot be much different from that of the American's.[1] Probably few families spend less

and below £160, and the percent of those earning less than £160 in each minor group, is shown in the following table. *Jour. Royal Stat. Soc.,* lxxiv, p. 66.

SALARIED EMPLOYEES—MEN AND LADS

Profession	Over £160.	Under £160.	Under £40.	£40–£60.	£60–£80.	£80–£100.	£100–£120.	£120–£140.	£140–£160.
Teachers 14 Counties W. Eng..	7,000	30,000	13	6	13	12	22	22	12
41 Boroughs W. Eng.	....	....	13	5	9	16	18	17	22
Scotch	1,500	4,500	2	2	4	16	25	24	27
Bankers	5,744	8,490	14	13	13	14	14	14	18
Insurance	1,619	1,585	21	18	12	12	15	10	12
Railway	2,440	26,874	10	13	26	22	15	8	6
Local Government London....			0	1	1	17	28	23	30
30 Eng. and Welsh Boroughs.	8,000	26,000	13	9	16	18	19	13	12
7 Scotch			9	8	13	17	24	15	14
Central Govt. Eng. and Wales.			8	14	14	17	17	17	13
Scotland	36,000	26,000	8	15	15	23	17	16	6
Ireland			10	13	16	21	18	14	8
Average	......	......	14	12	18	18	16	12	10

[1] *Bulletin of the Bureau of Labor,* no. 93, p. 555. According to these ratios, the proportion of income spent for rent averages one-tenth more in England than in America. That is, if the American spends 20 per cent of his income for housing, the Englishman spends 22 per cent.

TABLE XIV

RENTAL VALUES OF HOUSES IN ENGLAND AND SCOTLAND [1]

I.	II.	III.	IV.	V.	VI.
Annual rental value.		Number of houses.		Per cent.	
£.	$.	Metropolis.	England and Scotland.	Metropolis.	England and Scotland.
Separate dwellings (not taxed)		59,663	72,044	9.64	.91
Houses of annual value					
Under 10 .... Under 48.67		6,654	3,175,388	1.07	40.15
10 but under 20.. 48.67 but under 97.33..		116,103	3,121,009	18.75	39.47
Total, tax- exempt		182,420	6,368,441	29.46	80.53
Separate dwellings (taxed)					
20 but under 41.. 97.33 but under 199.53		12,631	15,100	2.04	.19
41 " 61. 199.53 " 296.87		4,678	5,129	.76	.06
Private dwelling houses					
20 but under 25 97.33 but under 121.67		96,876	406,034	15.65	5.13
25 " 30 121.67 " 146.00		57,999	268,537	9.37	3.40
30 " 41 146.00 " 199.53		127,601	426,843	20 61	5.40
41 " 50 199.53 " 243.67		40,137	104,531	6.48	1.32
50 " 61 243.67 " 296.87		37,922	126,068	6.13	1.59
61 " 100 296.87 " 486.67		28,666	100,925	4.63	1.28
100 and over .... 486.67 and over......		30,189	86,782	4.87	1.10
Total, taxed		436,699	1,539,949	70.54	19.47
Total, tax-exempt		182,420	6,368,441	29 46	80.53
Total, taxed and tax-exempt.......		619,119	7,908,390	100.00	100.00

[1] Compiled from material on pp. 80, 88, and 97 of the *Fifty-fourth Report of the Commissioners of His Majesty's Inland Revenue, for the year ended March 31st, 1911.* The figures relate to the fiscal year 1909-1910, and include dwellings and farm laborers' houses, but omit residential shops, lodging-houses, hotels, public houses, and coffee-houses, *some* of which should be included for a strictly inclusive presentation.

than a seventh of their revenue for shelter. On this supposition eighty per cent of the English families have incomes under £140 ($681), ninety per cent, under £210
($1,022).[1]

On the strength of the preceding survey, the following
conclusions may be confidently advanced:

1. The best attempts to estimate the distribution of incomes in the United States have been inconclusive.

2. There is a striking similarity between Spahr's description of the distribution of incomes in the United States, and
Leroy-Beaulieu's figures for Paris.

3. The Prussian and British income taxes are not a satisfactory guide to the distribution of revenues in those countries, although for incomes over 900 M., the Prussian impost, ignoring the possibility of extensive evasion, is, so far
as individuals are concerned, an excellent criterion.

4. The available data certainly indicate that a large number of families in each of the four greatest nations must
exist on very small incomes.

5. As far as money incomes are concerned, Americans
seem to be somewhat better off than Germans, French, or
English, but, in view of the differences in cost of living and
in mentality, it is unsafe to attempt to compare " welfare "
in the different countries.

6. Professor Nearing has shown that to form the base
of a general estimate of the distribution of incomes from
labor in the United States, American statistics are inadequate.

---

[1] The use of exact ratios such as may be found in the *Eighteenth
Annual Report of the Commissioner of Labor*, pp. 582, 585; or Chapin,
Standard of Living, p. 70, would give a misleading impression of precision. The value of classified rents as a guide to the distribution of
incomes will be discussed later, Chapter IX.

CHAPTER VI

Statistics of the Distribution of Wages

In the preceding chapters it has developed that data for an accurate description of the distribution of incomes or of earnings in the United States do not exist, and that the two most ambitious and scientific estimates have been unsatisfactory. It remains to consider just what inferences the published statistics warrant.

The first question to demand attention is, " Who support the families of the United States? " In 1900 there were 15,963,965 private families. There were 29,073,233 individuals, ten years of age or over, engaged in gainful occupations, of whom not more than 13,956,314 were married men; 9,797,522 were single males, and 5,319,397 were females. Therefore, there were at least 2,007,651 more families than there were wage-earning married men; that is, two million households were without what is generally considered the natural support and protector.[1] The average number of gainfully-employed persons per family was 1.82. In these figures, however, there is no hint of the number of men who bear unaided the financial burden of maintaining their households. A first approximation may be obtained as follows: Of the 25,440 families investigated by the Bureau of Labor in 1901, 95.92 per cent were to some extent dependent on the husband for support. To the total household income the wife contributed in 8.54 per cent, children in 22.19 per cent, boarders and lodgers in 23.26

---

[1] *Abstract of the Twelfth Census,* pp. 20, 24.

per cent, and other resources in 14.35 per cent of the cases.[1]
The sum of these percents is 68.34, but 4.08 per cent of
these families had no aid whatsoever from the father, leaving a maximum of 64.26 per cent of the households having
income from two sources.   In other words, if the sources
of income had been distributed so as to give as many families as possible a revenue from more than one contributor,
the expenses of 35.74 per cent would have been entirely de-
frayed by the father.   In 1890, 4,319 households dependent
upon the cotton, woolen, and glass industries were studied
by the same office.   It was found that in the cotton com-
munity 23.1 per cent of the families represented were supported solely by the husbands' exertions, 49.6 per cent in
the woolen, and 64.1 in the glass, or 40.6 per cent in all.[2]
It should be noted that these industries employ a large proportion of women and children.   Dr. Chapin found that
46.8 per cent of the households with incomes of from $600
to $1,099 in New York City, which came under his obser-
vation, were entirely maintained by the father.[3]   In view
of these facts is it not safe to conclude that certainly four-
tenths, probably forty-five per cent of industrial families,
are completely dependent on the father-husband?

It is not necessary to leave the question here, however,
for there exist some data which throw light on the problem.
In compiling Table XV, the original budgets of 391 families, prepared in 1907 for the Charity Organization Society
and described in Dr. Chapin's *Standard of Living in New
York City,* were used.   Table XVI is based upon the individual accounts of industrial families printed in the 1888
report of the New Jersey Bureau of Statistics of Labor

---

[1] *Eighteenth Annual Report of the Commissioner of Labor,* p. 362.
[2] Streightoff, *Standard of Living,* p. 59.
[3] Chapin, *Standard of Living,* p. 55.

TABLE XV

TOTAL FAMILY INCOME AND EARNINGS OF FATHER, 391 NEW YORK CITY FAMILIES, 1907

I. II. III. IV. V. VI. VII. VIII. IX. X. XI. XII. XIII. XIV. XV. XVI. XVII. XVIII. XIX. XX. XXI. XXII. XXIII. XXIV.

Earnings of father	Family incomes																			Family income			Families per 1000, father not sole support
	$400–499	$500–599	$600–699	$700–799	$800–899	$900–999	$1,000–1,099	$1,100–1,199	$1,200–1,299	$1,300–1,399	$1,400–1,499	$1,500–1,599	$1,600–1,699	$1,700–1,799	$1,800–1,899	$1,900–1,999	$2,000–2,099	$2,100–2,199	Total	In different group from father's	Larger than father's in same group	Total	
$100–$199						1						1							1	1		1	1000
200–299						1						1							1	1		1	1000
300–399	1	1	1	2	1	1													7	7		7	1000
400–499	7	2	4	5	5	1	2	1											27	20		20	740
500–599		15	14	9	9	2	2	1			1								53	38	4	42	793
600–699			52	20	12	6	5	2	1		1								99	47	10	57	576
700–799				44	21	8	9	3		2				1					87	43	4	47	540
800–899					24	12	1												37	13	4	17	460
900–999						32	6	5	2	2									47	15	1	16	340
1,000–1,099							9		1	2									12	3	1	4	333
1,100–1,199								4										1	5	1		1	200
1,200–1,299									4										4				0
1,300–1,399										2		1	1	1			1		6	4		4	666
1,400–1,499													1						1	1		1	1000
1,500–1,599												3	1						4	1		1	250
Totals	8	18	71	80	72	62	34	16	8	8	2	6	3	1			1	1	391	195	24	219	560

TABLE XVI

FAMILY INCOMES AND EARNINGS OF FATHERS[1]

I.	II.	III.	IV.	V.	VI.	VII.	VIII.	IX.	X.	XI.	XII.	XIII.	XIV.	XV.	XVI.	XVII.	XVIII.	XIX.	XX.	XXI.	XXII.	XXIII.	XXIV.
Earnings of father.	Family income.																			Family incomes.			
	$200-299	$300-399	$400-499	$500-599	$600-699	$700-799	$800-899	$900-999	$1,000-1,099	$1,100-1,199	$1,200-1,299	$1,300-1,399	$1,400-1,499	$1,500-1,599	$1,600-1,699	$1,700-1,799	$1,800-1,899	$1,900-1,999	Total.	In different group from father's.	Larger than father's in same group.	Total.	Families per 1000, father not sole support.
$100–$199	2	2	1																5	5		5	1000
200– 299	9	4	7	3	2	1		1											27	18		18	667
300– 399		50	15	16	7	5	4	2											104	54	6	60	576
400– 499			68	17	17	11	12	5		3									134	66	6	72	537
500– 599				58	13	8	6	4	1	2									95	37	4	41	432
600– 699					70	14	11	4	1	2									107	37	2	39	364
700– 799						52	10	5	3	1	4								80	28	6	34	425
800– 899							31	3	5	2	3	1							40	9	1	9	225
900– 999								19	4	3	1	1							27	8		8	333
1,000–1,099									19	2	1	1							27	8		9	296
1,100–1,199										8	1	3	1						17	9			529
1,200–1,299											10	5	1						12	2		1	250
1,300–1,399												2	1						3				333
1,400–1,499													1						0				
1,500–1,599														1	1				2				500
1,600–1,699																			0				
1,700–1,799																	1		0				
1,800–1,899																		1	1	1		1	1000
Totals....	11	56	91	94	109	91	74	43	38	23	22	13	4	4	4	0	3	1	681	284	26	310	455

[1] *Eleventh Annual Report Bureau of Statistics of Labor and Industries, New Jersey,* 1888, p. 376 ff.—Compiled.

and Industries. Since the number of families considered is in each case so small, it is not surprising to find irregularity. Nevertheless each table reveals a definite tendency for the proportion of families dependent solely upon the father to increase as his wages become larger. In the metropolis 44.0 per cent of all the households, and in New Jersey 54.5 per cent, were supported entirely by the exertion of the husband. The columns numbered IV and V in Table XVII show very conclusively that the greater the earning capacity of the father the less is the probability that his contribution will have to be supplemented from other sources. The apparent inconsistency between these two columns is probably due to the lapse of time, the rise in general prices, the difference in locality, and perhaps to other causes.

The New Jersey figures show that approximately fifty-five per cent of the households having husbands are entirely supported by them; it will be remembered that the number of private families is about one-seventh larger than the number of married men. If that ratio held in New Jersey in 1888, then, roughly, forty-eight per cent of the households were dependent on fathers.[1] In New York City, in 1907, the ratio would have been 38.31 per cent. It seems, therefore, safe to conclude that between four and five-tenths of the industrial families of the United States derive their entire money income from the labor of the father-husband.[2]

---

[1] $681 \times \frac{8}{7} = 778 : 681 - 310 = 371 : 371$ is 47.69% of 778.

[2] It should be noted that after the earnings of the father reach a certain point where saving is possible, the probability that he will invest begins to increase. The larger his labor income, the more able he is to set aside. So, if columns IV and V of Table XVII were continued, the values would presently begin to increase, and would doubtless ultimately reach and remain at 1.000. In other words, 100 per cent of the men with very high earnings, probably, have supplemental incomes from some form of capital.

TABLE XVII

VARIATION OF PROBABILITY THAT HUSBAND'S EARNINGS WILL BE SUPPLEMENTED, WITH RESPECT TO HIGH LIMIT OF HUSBAND'S EARNINGS [1]

I.	II.	III.	IV.	V.	VI.	VII.
	681 New Jersey families. 1888.				391 New York families. 1907.	
Husband's earnings under	Husband's earnings less than sum in column I.	Number of families having income greater than husband's earnings.	Probability that if husband's earnings are below sum in column I, family will have a supplementary income. New Jersey.	New York.	Number of families having income greater than husband's earnings.	Husband's earnings less than sum in column I.
$200	5	5	1.000	1.000	1	1
300	32	23	.719	1.000	2	2
400	136	83	.610	1.000	9	9
500	270	155	.574	.806	29	36
600	365	196	.537	.798	71	89
700	472	235	.498	.681	128	188
800	552	269	.487	.636	175	275
900	592	278	.470	.616	192	312
1,000	619	287	.464	.579	208	359
1,100	646	295	.457	.571	212	371
1,200	663	304	.459	.567	213	376
1,300	675	307	.455	.561	213	380
1,400	678	308	.454	.562	217	386
1,500	678	308	.454	.563	218	387
1,600	680	309	.455	.560	219	391
1,900	681	310	.455	....	....	....

[1] Perhaps columns IV and V of Table XVII will be clearer if it is noted that, if the decimal point were moved two places to the right, the figures in these columns would denote the percent of families having supplementary incomes if the father-husband's earnings are below the amount in column I.

This means that, not including the agricultural population, from four to five million men have each the entire financial responsibility of a home.[1]

The following presentation of statistics of the distribution of incomes cannot make practical recognition of these facts, because most of the published data fail to separate married from unmarried men, and, in addition, even did the distinction exist, these conclusions are too indefinite to permit of mathematical application. The discussion will, moreover, be confined mainly to the earnings of men. This is done for two reasons: first, if an attempt were made to cover the entire field of wage statistics, the essay would be unprofitably prolonged, it being impossible, in the present state of information, to combine the wages of men, women, and children, and thus to develop an approximation of family earnings; second, it is assumed that, in an ideal state, every male of marriageable age would be given a LIVING WAGE, by which is meant an earned income sufficient both to maintain the physical and mental efficiency of every member of a normal family and also to provide for the common emergencies of life—accident, sickness, unemployment, and old age. The first reason needs no defense, the second, perhaps, does. To maintain that society would be better off if all women were productively employed, child rearing in the home not being considered productive labor, is certainly plausible. Doubtless, a large proportion of

[1] Of 864 families having children at work in the glass industry, 314, or 36.3 per cent, were households in which economic *necessity* compelled the parents to send their children to the factories. Other motives for child labor were probably just as important as the need of their earnings, particularly the desire to have boys learn a trade. Thus other elements than the ability of the father as a provider enter into the causation of work by other members of the family. See the *Report on the Condition of Woman and Child Wage-Earners*, vol. iii, pp. 586, 587.

mothers are so unfit to train their offspring, that it might really be wise to entrust *all* children to the care of specialists, perhaps in the day nursery, perhaps continually. This would free the mother to aid in increasing the world's stock of good things, permit the preparation of food by expert dieticians, and give every girl and boy the advantage of the latest material appliances, prompt medical attention, and excellent discipline. The success of Sparta in wholesale public training of youth is an indisputable fact, and it is equally true that Daniel was reared, at least from the later years of childhood, as a ward of the state. Although this argument is reasonable, and in some ways attractive, it does not necessarily carry conviction. The modern tendency in caring for dependent children seems to be all the other way: the " cottage plan " has largely discredited the large asylum with one building; the " placing-out system " seems more and more to be winning its way. There appears to be scientific recognition of the need of the child for " mothering ", not as a matter of sentiment, but as a requirement of its mental and moral health. Now, if the mother is to care for her young children, the father must be earning enough to support the family during a period of several years: as men are made, it would be nonsense to say that each should have accumulated enough before marriage to tide him through these years, and at any rate, he should also be saving against the sickness almost sure to come eventually, or against old age. State aid to mothers with dependent children would tend to put a premium upon improvidence, and might entail some of the evil consequences of the old English Poor Law. The policy of paying larger wages to married than to single men, while idealistic, would very probably cause employers to give the preference to bachelors, and thus indirectly encourage prostitution. On the other hand, the wholesale or public care of children will not, in all likelihood, be undertaken, before Socialism has made considerable progress.   Thus whatever the merits of this question of child rearing, *for society as at present organized,* it is not an irrational ideal that every man should receive at least a LIVING WAGE.[1] For these two reasons, therefore, this study is confined to the earnings of men.

Before examining the latest statistics, it may be well to note the progress that has recently been made in raising pay.   Reliable wage data have not been published for many decades, but there is an extremely interesting set of figures in the volume containing the report of the New York State Census of 1865.   The number of men engaged in manufactures receiving each an amount from eight to a hundred twenty-eight dollars a month is given separately for each county and for the commonwealth.   The rule for the enumerators required that, if board was given as part of the compensation, its value should be added to the money wages in computing the pay.   Since there is a marked concentration upon multiples of five, and especially of ten dollars, in the following summary table, the monthly remuneration is given in five-dollar groups having multiples of five as their centers.

[1] For an argument for the Living Wage, see Professor John A. Ryan's book, *A Living Wage.*

TABLE XVIII

MONTHLY WAGES OF MEN IN MANUFACTURES, NEW YORK STATE, 1865 [1]

I.	II.	III.	IV.
Monthly wages.	Number of men.	Monthly wages.	Number of men.
$8–$12...........	108	$78–$82	2,475
13– 17..........	255	83– 87	1,381
18– 22..........	2,673	88– 92	274
23– 27..........	3,361	93– 97	177
28– 32..........	6,514	98–102	767
33– 37	9,437	103–107	....
38– 42..........	14,781	108–112	273
43– 47..........	8,555	113–117	60
48– 52..........	15,866	118–122	173
53– 57..........	4,944	123–127	10
58– 62..........	8,063	128–132	2
63– 67..........	4,536		
68– 72	2,850		
73– 77..........	1,427	Total	88,962

For the sake of comparison, the results of the federal
Census of Manufactures in 1904 are presented, the returns
covering 40 per cent of the wage-earners in the factories of
the State in that year.

TABLE XIX

WEEKLY WAGES OF MEN IN MANUFACTURES, SIXTEEN YEARS AND OVER,
NEW YORK STATE, 1904 [2]

I.	II.	III.	IV.
Wage group.	Number of men.	Wage group.	Number of men.
Less than $3	5,007	$10–$12	49,574
$3–$4	7,174	12– 15	57,275
4– 5	9,742	15– 20	51,666
5– 6	11,403	20– 25	16,574
6– 7	15,534	25 and over	9,300
7– 8	21,706		
8– 9	23,450		
9–10	39,985	Total	318,390

[1] *New York State Census*, 1865, pp. 512 *et seq.*, compiled.

[2] *Census of Manufactures*, 1905, pt. iv, p. 743.

From the earlier figures, it appears that the mean wage in New York in 1865 for the men engaged in manufactures was $48.19 per month, or $11.09 per week. In 1904, the average weekly pay for males, sixteen years of age and over, was $11.79.[1] These averages, however, cannot be accepted without qualification. In 1865, the men were probably paid in greenbacks which were worth, in gold, about 0.636 of their face value. At that rate $11.09 in greenbacks would buy as much as $7.05 in gold, but, since Falkner's index number of prices was 100.3 for 1865, and 93.3 for 1904, the $11.09 earned weekly by the operative in 1865 had a purchasing power equal to only $6.57 in 1904.[2] If Falkner's index number of greenback prices be used, the value of the weekly wage of 1865 is reduced still further to $4.77,[3] in purchasing power in 1904. This much, at least, is certain—in forty years, the average real wages of male factory operatives in New York State increased over eighty per cent.[4]

Has this improvement in remuneration been continuous up to the present time, or has it ceased during the last two decades? The Bureau of Labor index number of wages (full-time weekly earnings per employee) was 101.0 for 1890, 104.1 for 1900, and 112.2 for 1904, rising to 122.4 in 1907, the last year for which it was made public.[5] The purchasing power of full-time weekly earnings, measured by retail prices of food was 98.6 in 1890, 103.0 in 1900,

---

[1] *Census of Manufactures*, 1905, pt. iv, p. 670.

[2] Johnson, *Money and Currency*, pp. 112, 279.

[3] $11.09 \times \dfrac{93.3}{216.8} = 4.77.$

[4] It is possible that some allowance should be made for boys under sixteen included in the 1865 figures. The caption, however, reads "Men," and nothing is said of "Children" in those pages of the New York report.

[5] *Statistical Abstract of the United States*, 1908, p. 233.

100.4 in 1904, and 101.5 in 1907. These figures would seem to indicate that, although the general tendency of money wages to increase has not been seriously checked, there was no great gain in purchasing power. This index number, however, was not constructed in the most desirable manner, the system of weighting being open to criticism. It would, therefore, be well to seek other evidence. In 1907, Professor Henry L. Moore made a summary of the wage statistics of thirty of the industries treated in the *Dewey Report*. The following table presents a condensation of his results compared with those of the 1905 *Census of Manufactures*.

TABLE XX

WAGES IN MANUFACTURES IN THE UNITED STATES, CLASSIFIED WEEKLY EARNINGS
OF MALES SIXTEEN YEARS AND OVER [1]

I.	II.	III.	IV.	V.	VI.	VII.
	Numbers			Per cents.		
Wage group.	1890.	1900.	1904.	1890.	1900.	1904.
Less than $3 ..	444	591	56,346	.42	.37	2.2
$3–$4..........	2,329	2,646	57,597	2.22	1.66	2.2
4– 5..........	3,723	4,331	87,739	3.55	2.71	3.4
5– 6..........	2,735	3,880	103,429	2.61	2.43	4.0
6– 7..........	6,435	7,926	161,940	6.13	4.95	6.2
7– 8..........	9,529	15,727	196,981	9.10	9.83	7.5
8– 9..........	8,184	12,223	207,954	7.80	8.27	7.9
9–10..........	12,372	23,686	343,812	11.79	14.80	13.1
10–12..........	18,750	25,375	409,483	17.37	15.83	15.6
12–15..........	18,234	31,403	450,568	17.38	19.62	17.2
15–20	15,422	23,384	385,647	14.70	14.61	14.7
20–25..........	3,913	4,427	106,046	3.73	2.78	4.0
25 and over ...	2,853	3,446	51,511	2.70	2.14	2.0
Totals	104,923	160,055	2,619,053	100.00	100.00	100.0
Averages ...	$11.57	$11.52	$11.16			

[1] 1890 and 1900 figures give wage rates, as compiled by H. L. Moore from the *Dewey Report, Political Science Quarterly*, vol. xxii, pp. 66, 67; 1904 figures from *Census of Manufactures*, 1905, pt. iv, p. 645— show earnings, not rates.

Professor Moore's work revealed the startling truth that between 1890 and 1900 the average rate of pay, in the identical establishments which furnished the data for the *Dewey Report,* actually decreased from $11.57 to $11.52. He further showed that the standard deviation had decreased from 5.309 to 5.017, and the coefficient of variation from 45.9 to 43.5.[1] That the mean of 1904 should be less than that of 1900 is not surprising, because the *Dewey Report* presented rates of wages, the later *Census,* actual earnings. Nevertheless, in the face of these facts, it would be absurd to hold that there has been any marked increase in the money wages of males employed in manufacturing between 1890 and 1904, the most recent year for which general statistics are available. Using the data in Column IV of Table XIX, a rough average of $11.46 is obtained, a standard deviation of 5.12 and a coefficient of variation of 44.7. This approximate coefficient of variation would seem to indicate a lessened tendency to concentrate about the mean. Although these constants for the latest year are not precisely determined, they are not far wrong, for the same tendency can be observed in the distribution as shown in the table: for instance, in 1890, 2.64 per cent; in 1900, 2.03, and in 1904, 4.4 were earning less than $4 per week. The corresponding percents for those receiving less than $10 per week were 43.62, 45.02, and 46.5; for those paid less than $12 per week they were 61.49, 60.85, and 62.1; and for those receiving $20 or more, the percents were 6.43 in 1890, 4.92 in 1900, and 6.0 in 1904. The conclusion, then, seems warranted that between 1890 and 1904 there was no perceptible increase of the average money wages of male factory operatives, and that for the first decade of the

[1] The standard deviation and the coefficient of variation are measures of distribution about the mean. The smaller these are, the more are the earnings concentrated about some point.

period there was a tendency for wage rates to concentrate
about the mean, a trend which, in the next five years, was
probably reversed.[1]

In contrast to these figures for the nation as a whole, the
proportion of men in factories earning less than $8 per
week, fell between 1897 and 1908 from 36.0 to 17.4 per
cent in New Jersey, and from 32.2 to 13.5 in Massachusetts; likewise, the percent of those receiving less than $12
per week decreased from 68.1 to 56.7 in the former and
from 67.7 to 51.7 in the latter commonwealth.[2]   Thus, the
decline being almost regular, it would appear that in these
two important industrial states there has been an actual
improvement in the distribution of money wages of the
men engaged in manufacture.   It is impossible to determine the change in average weekly pay in these two states,
but it is certain that the average annual earnings of all
employees in the factories of Massachusetts have been considerably augmented.[3]   In New York, the index number
for per diem compensation of all organized working men
increased from 96 in 1897 to 119 in 1908, and for half-
year's earnings, from 93 to 111.   Although these averages
are unweighted, they cannot misrepresent the general tendency, for only four trades, cloth hat and cap makers,
cloak makers, longshoremen, and machine wood-workers,
suffered a decrease in the average daily wage during this

---

[1] It must not be forgotten that these conclusions deal with money
rates and earnings only.   The purchasing power of money fell in this
period.   On the other hand, no figures have been given for the age
composition of the operating forces of the establishments considered at
these different periods.   A change in this, or in the ratio of skilled to
unskilled laborers might materially affect the average wage rates without changing the pay for a given kind of work.

[2] Streightoff, *Standard of Living*, Appendix A and B; also chart,
p. 53.

[3] *Ibid.*, p. 47.

period. In nearly every occupation both the average daily and the average half-yearly earnings were higher in 1904 than in 1897 or in 1900.[1] During 1907, half-yearly earnings were at a maximum, 122, daily wages being 118. Between 1897 and 1907, the Bureau of Labor index of retail prices of food rose from 96.3 to 120.6. Thus, in these ten years, daily money wages increased an average of 23 per cent, retail food prices 25 per cent, and half-yearly money earnings 31 per cent. A computation combining these percents would be inexact because the index number of New York wages is not a weighted average, and because the relative prices of food represent the country as a whole; food prices for the North Atlantic States increased 23 per cent.[2]

[1] New York, *Annual Report of the Bureau of Labor Statistics*, 1908, pt. ii, pp. xxiii, xxviii *et seq.*

[2] *Statistical Abstract of the United States*, 1908, p. 558. The Bureau of Labor index of retail food prices was discontinued after 1907. As to wholesale prices, not a completely reliable guide to retail prices, the general index rose from 1897 to 1910, from 89.7 to 131.6, or 46.7 per cent. In the same period wholesale prices of food rose from 87.7 to 128.7, or 46.8 per cent. (*Bulletin of the Bureau of Labor*, no. 93, pp. 318, 321.)

In this period the index of daily wages in New York rose from 96 to 124, or about 29 per cent, and the index of quarterly earnings from 94 to 124, or about 32 per cent. (See Table XXIX in this essay.)

The following table shows the latest wage data published by the Interstate Commerce Commission. Column V shows the increase in the average wages for each occupation, and column VI reduces this increase to per cents. From 1900 to 1910 wholesale prices for all commodities in the United States rose from 110.5 to 131.6, or 19.1 per cent; wholesale food prices rose from 104.2 to 128.7, or 23.5 per cent. The average wages in seven branches of railway service, now embracing 601,000 men, rose less than 19.1 per cent. In each of thirteen occupations, embracing 1,208,000 employees (in 1910) it rose less than 23.5 per cent. These figures tempt rash interpretations, but it is at least safe to say that the daily wages of railway employees have not increased much faster than the cost of living; perhaps they have fallen off a little in purchasing power. It is interesting to note that, except for the " switch-tenders, crossing-tenders and watchmen," the least increase was that in

To sum up, then, the Bureau of Labor index number shows a rise of three per cent in average full-time weekly money wages from 1890 to 1900, of eleven per cent from 1890 to 1904, and of twenty-one per cent from 1890 to 1907, while the purchasing power of these wages rose four

the pay of "general office clerks." There may be a tendency to employ women in this work.

COMPENSATION OF EMPLOYEES OF THE RAILWAYS OF THE UNITED STATES, SHOWING INCREASE OF DAILY WAGES, 1900 TO 1910[1]

I.	II.	III. IV.		V. VI.	
Class.	Number.	Average daily compensation.		Increase in average daily compensation, 1900 to 1910.	
	1910.	1910.	1900.	Dollars.	Per cent.
General officers	5,476	$13 27	$10.45	$2.82	27.0
Other officers	9,392	6,22	5.22	1.00	19.2
General office clerks	76,329	2.40	2.19	.21	9.6
Station agents	37,379	2.12	1.75	.37	21.1
Other station men	153,104	1.84	1.60	.24	15.0
Enginemen	64,691	4.55	3.75	.80	21.3
Firemen	68,321	2.74	2.14	.60	28.0
Conductors	48,682	3.91	3.17	.74	23.3
Other trainmen	136,938	2.69	1.96	.73	37.2
Machinists	55,193	3.08	2.30	.78	33.9
Carpenters	68,085	2.51	2.04	.47	23.0
Other shopmen	225,196	2.18	1.73	.45	26.0
Section foremen................	44,207	1.99	1.68	.31	18.4
Other trackmen................	378,955	1.47	1.22	.25	20.5
Switch tenders, crossing tenders and watchmen	44,682	1.69	1.80	—.11	—6.1
Telegraph operators and dispatchers	42,435	2.33	1.96	.37	18.9
Employees—account floating equipment....................	10,549	2.22	1.92	.30	15.6
All other employees and laborers .	229,806	2.01	1.71	.30	17.5
Totals	1,699,420	..	..	....	....

[1] *Statistics of the Railways* for year ending June 30, 1910, pp. 33, 38.

and a half, two, and three per cent respectively for these
intervals. On the other hand, the *Dewey Report* and the
Census of Manufactures of 1905 indicate an actual decrease of the average money compensation of factory workmen, and, because more concentrated about the mean, a
somewhat less favorable distribution of earnings. The statistics of Massachusetts and of New Jersey make it evident
that in these two states, each year a smaller proportion of
men are in the low-wage groups. There was a considerable
rise, in the decade ending 1907, of the average daily and
half-yearly earnings of the organized workmen of New
York; yet in purchasing power of food, it is doubtful if
these daily wages have increased at all; in value, the half-
yearly labor incomes may have gained five per cent, but
from 1897 to 1910 they probably decreased. The evidence
is, therefore, conflicting; [1] but it points surely to the conclusion that there was no great improvement in the money
compensation of factory operatives between 1890 and 1904,
and that if there has been an increase of the pay of workmen in late years, it has been largely, if not entirely, offset
by rapidly rising prices.

The reason for this searching inquiry into the truth of
the prevalent belief that there was a large increase in wages
during the last two decades, is to show clearly that, in so
far as labor earnings are an index, there is no ground
for believing that these years witnessed any startling
change in the distribution of incomes. From the fact,
then, that certain statistics were compiled in 1900, or
in 1904, it does not inevitably follow that they grossly misrepresent the state of affairs in 1912. On the other hand,

---

[1] The factor of unemployment has not been considered. Unemployment seems to be periodic: it varies widely from year to year, but it
would be difficult to show that it has been growing any less burden-
some of late. See reports of the New York Bureau of Labor Statistics,
especially *Bulletin, Department of Labor*, no. 48, Sept. 1911, p. 344.

it cannot be maintained that the figures of the Twelfth
Census are truly typical of the present. The only excuse
for presenting data now over ten years old, is that nothing
more recent is available, and that, as long as its true character is recognized, approximate knowledge is better than
absolute ignorance.

In the field of manufactures, the Census of 1905 furnishes the most recent data of general scope. Table XXI
exhibits the distribution of weekly earnings among males,
aged sixteen years or over, engaged in this branch of industry in the United States in 1904:

TABLE XXI[1]

CLASSIFIED WEEKLY EARNINGS OF MALES, SIXTEEN YEARS AND OVER, ENGAGED IN
MANUFACTURE IN THE UNITED STATES IN 1904

I.	II.	III.	IV.	V.	VI.	VII.
	Enumeration.			Estimate.		
		Percents.			Percents.	
Wage group.	Number.	Actual.	Cumulative.	Number.	Actual.	Cumulative.
Under $3	56,346	2.2	2.2	92,535	2.2	2.2
$3 but under $4	57,597	2.2	4.4	96,569	2.3	4.5
4 " " 5	87,739	3.4	7.8	149,531	3.5	8.0
5 " " 6	103,429	4.0	11.8	177,550	4.2	12.2
6 " " 7	161,940	6.2	18.0	272,288	6.4	18.6
7 " " 8	196,981	7.5	25.5	327,726	7.7	26.3
8 " " 9	207,954	7.9	33.4	336,669	7.9	34.2
9 " " 10	343,812	13.1	46.5	557,046	13.1	47.3
10 " " 12	409,483	15.6	62.1	654,435	15.4	62.7
12 " " 15	450,568	17.2	79.3	714,816	16.9	79.6
15 " " 20	385,647	14.7	94.0	609,797	14.4	94.0
20 " " 25	106,046	4.0	98.0	170,571	4.0	98.0
25 and over	51,511	2.0	100.0	84,005	2.0	100.0
Total	2,619,053	100.0		4,244,538	100.0	

[1] *Census of Manufactures*, 1905, pt. iv, pp. 645, 647.

If the estimate is more exactly representative of the conditions in the United States as a whole, than is the enumeration, the differences are trifling.   These figures show that over forty-six per cent of the men employed in factories were actually earning less than $10 per week, or $522 per annum; more than sixty per cent received less than $12 weekly or $626 in the year; on the other hand, some six per cent were so fortunate as to enjoy a weekly compensation of at least $20, or, for the twelve months, full-time earnings of $1,043.   Of these four million two hundred thousand men, in other words, in excess of two million six hundred thousand were laboring for compensation at a rate which in the year would have netted them under $626, and less than two hundred and sixty thousand would have received more than $1,043 if they had earned in every week as much as in the one represented in the Census returns. Two comments may be made on the interpretation of this statement: first, since the " busy week ", the week when the greatest number were employed in each establishment, was chosen for the enumeration, the count may have included an unusually large proportion of extra hands; these " extras " may have been mainly non-skilled workers, and, therefore, low paid; second, the remuneration of these " men " is not typical of the recompense of fathers of families.   The first observation is merely a surmise, the second expresses known facts.   The average wages of women in factories, mills, and stores reaches a maximum after sixteen years of service.[1]   Again, the compensation of males in the Massachusetts cotton factories attains a maximum at the age period forty-five to forty-nine, in North Carolina exactly twenty years earlier, but, in the southern state, the

---

[1] *Report on Condition of Women and Child Wage-Earners in the United States*, vol. v, pp. 42, 47; also vol. i, p. 314.

high rate continues over a decade. The average male factory operative does not begin to approach his full earning power until he passes his twentieth birthday. Doubtless a considerable number of these four million, two hundred thousand men were below the age of twenty, but since it is improbable that many of the youths had their own families, it is a safe inference that by the time a man is ready to marry, he should normally have passed beyond the lowest earnings groups. The truth of the statement seems to be in a measure confirmed by Table XXII. This table was

TABLE XXII

COMPARISON OF THE CLASSIFIED EARNINGS OF HEADS OF FAMILIES WITH CLASSI-
FIED WAGE RATES OF MALES SIXTEEN YEARS AND OVER, ALL FACTORY
EMPLOYEES

1901.			1900.		
Classified annual earnings of heads of families.			Classified weekly wage rates of males 16 years and over.		
I.	II.	III.	IV.	V.	VI.
Earnings.	Men.	Per cent.	Per cent.	Men.	Weekly wage rates.
Under $100	49	.32			
$100 or under $200 ..	134	.84	2.08	3,237	$2 but under $4
200 " 300 ..	431	2.72	5.27	8,211	4 " 6
300 " 400 ..	1,282	8.09	15.18	23,653	6 " 8
400 " 500 ..	2,602	16.43	23.69	36,919	8 " 10
500 " 600 ..	2,825	17.83	16.28	25,375	10 " 12
600 " 700 ..	2,774	17.51	16.27	25,357	12 " 14
700 " 800 ..	2,886	18.22	9.80	15,269	14 " 16
800 " 900 ..	1,135	7.16	5.18	8,075	16 " 18
900 " 1,000 ..	987	6.23	3.90	6,086	18 " 20
1000 or over.........	736	4.65	2.35	3,663	20 " 24
Totals	15,841	100.00	100.00	155,845	Under $24

constructed as follows: from the data in the *Eighteenth Annual Report of the Commissioner of Labor,* were selected those dealing with the distribution of annual earnings among the heads of households who were engaged in various branches of manufacture.[1] Thus, columns II and III were obtained. Since that study was confined to families having incomes under $1,200, the number of men earning $24 per week or over in Professor Moore's summary of the *Dewey Report* for 1900 [2] was subtracted from the total and the percents recalculated on this basis to give column IV. Columns II and IV are only roughly comparable because the wage rates are only approximately equivalent to the earnings groups; nevertheless, even without taking account of the losses caused by annual unemployment, the conclusion is inevitable that the pay of heads of families engaged in manufacture ranges higher than that of males over sixteen. The surprising fact is that the difference shown is not greater.

Probably the present trend of earnings in manufactures is best exhibited by a comparison of the most recent changes in classified wages.[3]

Table XXIII shows that for both Kansas and New Jersey, the two states for which the returns of the years 1904 and 1909 are strictly comparable, there has been a movement from the lower to the higher wage groups, the better-

[1] *Eighteenth Annual Report of the Commissioner of Labor,* p. 284.

[2] See Table XX.

[3] The figures for 1904 are taken from the *Census of Manufactures* for 1905, pt. iv, pp. 670, 746, and are all for men employed in manufactures, sixteen years or more of age. The figures for 1908 or 1909 are either taken, or calculated from data in the latest available reports of the respective state bureaus. Those for Massachusetts refer to males at least twenty-one years of age, those for New Jersey and Kansas to males at least sixteen, and those for Wisconsin to all males.

TABLE XXIII

WAGES OF MALES IN FOUR STATES, ENGAGED IN MANUFACTURES

Weekly Wages.	Per cents.								Cumulative per cents.							
	Massachusetts (21 years and over, 1908.)		New Jersey (16 years and over.)		Kansas (16 years and over.)		Wisconsin (All males, 1909)		Massachusetts (21 years and over.)		New Jersey (16 years and over.)		Kansas (16 years and over)		Wisconsin (All males, 1909)	
	1904.	1908.	1904.	1909.	1904.	1909.	1904.	1909.	1904.	1908.	1904.	1909.	1904.	1909.	1904.	1909.
Under $5....	5.	1.4	6.6	3.5	7.3	2.3	4.7	2.5	5.	1.4	6.6	3.5	7.3	2.3	4.7	2.5
$5-6........	4.2	1.8	3.4	3.0	2.4	1.2	2.6	.7	9.2	3.2	10.0	6.5	9.7	3.5	7.3	3.2
6-7.........	6.7	3.9	4.8	4.4	4.7	2.0	4.6	2.9	15.9	7.1	14.8	10.9	14.4	5.5	11.9	6.1
7-8.........	8.5	6.4	6.7	5.8	5.9	2.9	7.2	3.8	24.4	13.5	21.5	16.7	20.3	8.4	19.1	9.9
8-9.........	8.7	9.0	8.4	7.5	7.7	3.6	9.7	3.0	33.1	22.5	29.9	24.2	28.0	12.0	28.8	12.9
9-10........	12.2	11.8	12.4	14.4	13.6	14.5	18.7	19.2	45.3	34.3	42.3	38.6	41.6	26.5	47.5	32.1
10-12.......	15.8	17.6	15.6	16.6	22.1	20.0	20.2	22.2	61.1	51.9	57.9	55.2	63.7	46.5	67.7	54.3
12-15.......	18.1	20.1	16.9	17.7	17.9	23.5	17.5	23.1	79.2	72.0	74.8	72.9	81.6	70.0	85.2	77.4
15-20.......	15.8	20.0	18.0	17.8	12.5	20.7	11.5	18.1	95.0	92.0	92.8	90.7	94.1	90.7	96.7	95.5
20-25.......	3.5	5.6	4.8	5.9	3.5	6.6	2.5	3.3	98.5	97.6	97.6	96.6	97.6	97.3	99.2	98.8
25 and over .	1.5	2.4	2.4	5.4	2.4	2.7	.8	1.2	100.0	100.0	100.0	100.0	100.0	100.0	100.0	100.0
Totals	100.0	100.00	100.0	100.0	100.0	100.0	100.0	100.0								
Averages .	$11.15		$11.75		$11.22		$10.75	$12.06								
Number....	281,179	350,118	92,788	224,789	16,757	50,720	49,673	141,218								

ment being especially marked in Kansas. For instance, in
the younger commonwealth the proportion of men earning
less than $12 per week fell from 63.7 per cent to 46.5 per
cent, a truly remarkable change. In New Jersey the decrease of this proportion was from 57.9 to 55.2 per cent;
the greatest improvement in this state was the contraction
of the very lowest wage group. In view of the fact that
children under sixteen were included in the later Wisconsin
enumeration, her progress was particularly great; the figures for Massachusetts are incomparable, but it has already
been noted that earnings steadily increased in this commonwealth during the decade 1897 to 1907, and the 1908 figures show no retrogression. It is, then, safe to believe that,
had a general Census of Wages paid in Manufactures been
taken in 1910, it would have shown a considerable reduction
in the proportion of males earning less than $12 weekly;
the percent receiving more than $20 would have slightly in-
creased; the principal change seems to have been in the
direction of greater concentration of wages between $9 and
$20.

The statistics of wages of factory operatives clearly indicate, therefore, that in 1904 the maximum earning power
of sixty-two per cent of the adult males employed was
$626 per year, while, if they worked full time, six per cent
may have received upward of $1,043. Moreover, the labor
incomes of heads of families engaged in this branch of industry would range a little higher than those of adult males.
Finally, the last five years for which some state figures are
available, the period from 1904 to 1909 witnessed a general
increase of earnings, so that at the latter date the pay of
probably less than sixty per cent of the men was below $12
per week.

Annual earnings in manufacturing seem to be slightly
higher than those in other industrial pursuits. Evidence

for this exists in the *Eighteenth Annual Report of the Commissioner of Labor.*

TABLE XXIV[1]

CLASSIFIED ANNUAL EARNINGS OF HEADS OF FAMILIES, 1901

I.	II.	III.	IV.	V.	VI.	VII.	VIII.
	Per cent of heads of families in						
Annual earnings.	All	Manufacturers.	Non-manu-facturing industry.	Domestic and personal service.	Mining.	Trade.	Transportation.
Under $100..........	.37	.32	.48	1.34	..	.18	.22
$100–$200...........	1.11	.84	1.59	2.04	1.98	.58	.77
200– 300...........	3.02	2.72	3.56	5.57	6.73	2.53	2.02
300– 400...........	8.37	8.09	8.90	9.40	19.92	7.36	6.92
400– 500...........	16.79	16.43	17.45	15.97	26.52	17.79	16.73
500– 600...........	17.90	17.83	18.02	14.48	16.89	21.21	19.52
600– 700...........	17.86	17.51	18.50	17.32	10.95	20.98	20.17
700– 800...........	16.85	18.22	14.32	13.38	7.25	15.17	16.08
800– 900...........	6.17	7.16	4.34	5.08	3.16	3.73	4.41
900–1000...........	6.16	6.23	6.04	7.86	4.09	4.84	5.62
1000 or over	5.40	4.65	6.80	7.56	2.51	5.63	7.54
Men engaged	24,402	15,841	8,561	2,010	758	2,254	3,222

The above table indicates that the earnings of factory operatives are somewhat higher than those of men in all the other industries covered in this report. In transportation alone is there a greater percent of heads of families earning upward of $600 per annum. However, there is no very great difference in favor of manufacturing over trade. As far as this investigation of over twenty-four

[1] *Eighteenth Annual Report of the Commissioner of Labor,* pp. 284, 285, partly compiled.

thousand men is concerned the industrial workers seem to
be about equally well off in all of these three branches of industry.   However, as the canvass upon which this table is
based was confined to families with annual incomes below
$1,200, no dogmatic statement can safely be made.

Nevertheless, this investigation furnishes the most important published data upon the distribution of incomes in
the United States.   The summary of the results, so far as
they concern the annual earnings of men, presented in
Table XXIV, shows that, in 1901, 47.56 per cent of the
heads of families having incomes under $1,200 earned
less than $600 per annum, 34.71 per cent received $600
but less than $800, 12.33 per cent $800 and under $1,000,
and 5.40 per cent $1,000 or more.   These percentages prob-
ably do not greatly misrepresent the distribution of annual
earnings among mature industrial workmen, for although,
as has been pointed out, the study was confined to families
having incomes under $1,200, the fact that, whereas 12.33
per cent of the fathers were earning $800 and under $1,000,
only 5.40 per cent received $1,000 or more, is a pretty safe
indication that, in the occupations considered, the proportion of the total number of employees enjoying compensation above $1,200 was very small.   There are notable ex-
ceptions to this statement as a general proposition, particularly the railway engineers and conductors, yet in nineteen
of the fifty-five occupations represented by a minimum of
one hundred men, not a single individual earned over
$1,000, and in thirty-eight, less than four per cent re-
ceived more than that amount.   Moreover, in no published returns of classified wages in manufactures of all
those studied in the preparation of this essay, has the
proportion of adult males earning over $25 per week
exceeded four per cent, and both the *Dewey Report*
and the Wisconsin manufacturing returns show that

over two-thirds of the men so well paid receive under $35.[1] Finally, although six and a half per cent of the 681 men canvassed in New Jersey in 1888[2] earned between $1,000 and $1,200, the proportion receiving $1,200 or more was but 2.6 per cent, nearly three-fourths of whom were paid less than $1,300. In Dr. Chapin's study, 4.4 per cent of the men obtained for their labor from $1,000 to $1,200, and 3.2 per cent above that sum. It seems, therefore, reasonable to believe that Table XXV, which is a condensation of the data on earnings in this *Report of the Commissioner of Labor* is, except for certain occupations, fairly representative of the distribution of annual labor incomes among the heads of industrial families in the United States in 1901.

For some of the occupations represented in Table XXV, and for a few others the individual returns of annual earnings of working men in Kansas and Iowa as summarized in Tables XXVI and XXVII, offer later data. Table XXVI shows that, with the possible exception of eighteen individuals, who did not report on this subject, the 1,574 persons who filled out the Kansas questionnaires were members of labor unions. This would lead to the expectation that the wages would be higher than those compiled in the federal report, and such is the case. Moreover, the returns for the series of years show a tendency in almost all of the occupations, both in Iowa and in Kansas, for compensation to rise. The summary Table XXVIII may be said roughly to represent the approximate distribution of incomes and earnings among the workers in these occupations from 1903 to 1907 in Kansas, and from 1905 to 1909 in Iowa.

[1] Moore, "Variability of Wages," *Political Science Quarterly*, vol. xii, p. 67; *Fourteenth Annual Report, Bureau of Labor and Industrial Statistics*, Wisconsin, 1909-1910, pt. viii, p. 813.

[2] See Table XVII, p. 93.

TABLE XXV [1]

PER CENT OF HEADS OF FAMILIES IN EACH GROUP OF CLASSIFIED EARNINGS, IN
OCCUPATIONS EMBRACING 100 OR MORE PERSONS (CONDENSED)

Occupation.	Under $600.	$600 but under $800.	$800 but under $1,000.	$1,000 or over.
Bakers (food, etc.)	36.54	57.06	4.48	1.92
Barbers	41.79	53.73	3.73	.75
Bartenders	30.12	60.24	8.44	1.20
Blacksmiths (iron and steel)	24.75	41.59	31.68	1.98
Blacksmiths (vehicles)	27.53	48.55	20.29	3.63
Boilermakers	16.53	42.97	35.54	4.96
Brakemen (railroad)	37.50	52.72	9.78	....
Bricklayers	13.92	27.82	46.52	11.74
Butchers	47.94	44.63	4.13	3.30
Cabinet-makers	39.00	41.00	17.00	3.00
Carpenters (hand trades)	40.46	45.84	11.78	1.92
Carpenters (vehicles)	45.05	45.95	8.10	.90
Cigarmakers	48.11	39.46	10.27	2.16
Clerks (trade)	26.07	42.55	20.21	11.17
Clerks (transportation)	22.45	45.58	22.45	9.52
Coal miners	81.18	17.27	1.55	....
Compositors	21.42	38.69	25.60	14.29
Conductors (steam railway)	3.23	19.35	35.49	41.93
Conductors (street railway)	28.15	64.82	7.03	....
Drivers (trade)	72.13	27.47	.40	....
Drivers (transportation)	63.38	34.27	2.35	....
Engineers (locomotive)	1.56	11.85	28.86	57.73
Engineers (stationary)	20.00	42.73	26.36	10.91
Farm laborers	90.00	1.00	...	....
Firemen (locomotive)	22.38	58.04	12.59	6.99
Freight handlers	83.65	16.35	....	....
Hod-carriers	78.77	21.23	....	....
Janitors	60.30	34.35	3.82	1.53
Laborers (domestic and personal service)	93.49	6.51	....	....
Laborers (food, etc.)	93.39	6.61	....	....
Laborers (iron and steel)	92.30	7.70	....	....
Laborers (lumber)	96.18	3.82	....	....
Laborers (textiles)	99.33	.67	....	....
Laborers (vehicles)	91.89	8.11	....	....
Laborers (miscellaneous manufactures)	91.03	8.77	.20	....
Laborers (trade)	90.15	9.47	.38	....
Laborers (transportation)	84.80	15.20	....	....
Letter-carriers	6.86	8.82	49.02	35.30
Longshoremen	67.57	30.40	1.35	.68
Machinists (iron and steel)	14.72	57.67	24.70	2.91
Machinists (vehicles)	18.83	52.59	24.03	4.55
Masons	26.19	40.48	29.36	3.97
Molders	18.38	50.22	27.81	3.59
Motormen	36.15	59.04	4.81	....
Painters (hand trades)	45.35	41.57	10.93	2.15
Painters (vehicles)	43.24	45.04	10.82	.90
Plasterers	27.36	42.45	22.64	7.55
Plumbers	7.49	29.95	35.29	27.27
Policemen	5.00	26.66	45.84	22.50
Salesmen (grocery)	41.71	50.92	4.30	3.07
Section hands (railroad)	94.23	5.77	....	....
Stone cutters	18.92	33.11	39.86	8.11
Switchmen (railroad)	35.84	43.33	14.16	6.67
Tailors	54.32	30.45	10.15	5.08
Tinsmiths	36.07	54.09	8.20	1.64
All occupations (24,402 men)	47.56	34.71	12.33	5.40

[1] *Eighteenth Annual Report of the Commissioner of Labor*, pp. 283, 285.

TABLE XXVI

CLASSIFIED INCOMES FOR THE YEARS 1903, 1904, 1906, AND 1907, FAMILY
OBLIGATIONS AND ORGANIZATION MEMBERSHIP OF CERTAIN WAGE-
EARNERS IN KANSAS

Occupation.	Year.	Under $600.	$600 under $800.	$800 under $1,000.	$1,000 under $1,500.	$1,500 under $2,000.	$2,000 and over.	Totals.	Number of heads of families.	Number *not* members of unions.
Brakeman	1903	2	4	4	1	....	....	11	11	......
"	1904	1	4	1	....	....	....	6	4	(?) 1
"	1906	1	2	7	....	....	....	10	9	......
"	1907	....	1	6	1	....	....	8	8	......
Totals	....	4	11	18	2	....	....	35	32	(?) 1
Conductors	1903	....	....	1	13	2	....	16	12	......
"	1904	....	1	....	9	1	....	11	11	......
"	1906	....	....	2	11	5	....	18	18	......
"	1907	....	....	....	22	2	. ..	24	24	......
Totals	....	....	1	3	55	10	....	69	65	......
Engineers	1903	....	1	....	11	2	1	15	14	......
"	1904	....	2	....	5	3	1	11	10	......
"	1906	....	....	....	7	6	....	13	13	......
"	1907	1	....	....	5	4	....	10	10	......
Totals	....	1	3	....	28	15	2	49	47	......
Firemen	1903	2	3	1	1	....	....	7	3	......
"	1904	....	1	2	1	....	....	4	2	......
"	1905	2	4	7	1	....	....	14	10	......
"	1907	....	....	9	2	....	....	11	11	......
Totals	....	4	8	19	5	....	....	36	26	......
Carmen (car inspectors)	1903	6	7	1	....	....	....	14	14	......
"	1904	3	6	2	1	....	....	12	10	......
"	1906	8	16	....	....	....	....	25	23	......
"	1907	13	16	10	....	....	....	39	36	......
Totals	....	31	45	13	1	....	....	90	83	......

TABLE XXVI

CLASSIFED INCOMES FOR THE YEARS 1903, 1904, 1906, AND 1907, FAMILY
OBLIGATIONS AND ORGANIZATION MEMBERSHIP OF CERTAIN WAGE-
EARNERS IN KANSAS—*Continued*

Occupation.	Year.	Under $600.	$600 under $800.	$800 under $1,000.	$1,000 under $1,500.	$1,500 under $2,000.	$2,000 and over.	Totals.	Number of heads of families.	Number *not* members of unions.
Machinists	1903	....	1	8	4	....	....	13	13	......
"	1904	6	5	....	1	....	....	12	11	......
"	1906	....	....	6	10	....	....	16	15	......
"	1907	....	....	4	2	....	....	6	5	......
Totals	....	6	6	18	17	....	....	47	44	......
Other railroad employees including black-smiths, boilermakers, their helpers. iron molders (varying numbers)	1903	8	10	12	18	....	....	48	41	......
	1904	8	6	12	2	....	....	28	25	......
	1906	6	6	9	1	....	....	22	21	......
	1907	....	3	8	9	....	....	20	18	......
Totals	....	22	25	41	30	....	....	118	105	......
Bricklayers and stone-masons	1903	16	11	5	10	1	...	43	37	.....
"	1904	8	9	7	4	....	....	28	23	.....
"	1906	4	3	....	2	1	....	10	6	......
"	1907	3	5	9	1	1	....	19	19	......
Totals	....	31	28	21	17	3	....	100	85	......
Carpenters	1903	55	63	15	7	....	....	140	123	......
"	1904	17	11	7	....	....	....	35	34	......
"	1906	11	18	4	....	....	....	33	30	......
"	1907	13	35	16	1	....	....	65	57	......
Totals	...	96	127	42	8	....	....	273	244	......
Painters and paper-hangers	1903	13	13	3	1	....	....	30	21	......
"	1904	1	1	3	....	....	....	5	4	......
"	1906	2	3	....	....	....	....	5	5	......
"	1907	2	2	1	....	....	....	5	5	......
Totals	....	18	19	7	1	....	....	45	35	......

TABLE XXVI

CLASSIFIED INCOMES FOR THE YEARS 1903, 1904, 1906, AND 1907, FAMILY
OBLIGATIONS AND ORGANIZATION MEMBERSHIP OF CERTAIN WAGE-
EARNERS IN KANSAS— *Continued*

Occupation.	Year,	Under $600.	$600 under $800.	$800 under $1,000.	$1,000 under $1,500.	$1,500 under $2,000.	$2,000 and over.	Totals.	Number of heads of families.	Number *not* members of unions.
Barbers	1903	3	9	2	1			15	14	
"	1904		4	3				7	7	
"	1906	1	25	2	1			29	20	
"	1907	1	17	2				20	16	
Totals		5	55	9	2			71	57	
Cigarmakers	1903	8	4					12	10	
"	1904	8	2					10	10	
"	1906	10	4	4				18	12	
"	1907	8	13	1				22	12	
Totals		34	23	5				62	44	
Miners and mine em-	1903	55	34	12	1			102	79	
ployees	1904	44	15	6				65	61	
"	1906	28	9	3				40	32	
"	1907	16	10	5	2			33	27	
Totals		143	68	26	3			240	199	
Common laborers (1903	1903	68	9	3				80	77	
and 1904 classed with	1904	3	2					5	5	
building trades; 1907	1906									
with miscellaneous).	1907	7	5					12	6 (?) 12
Totals		78	16	3				97	88 (?) 12
Teamsters	1903	27	7	2	2			38	32	
"	1904	4	1					5	5	
"	1906	9	3					12	10	
"	1907	23	12					35	22	2
Totals		63	23	2	2			90	69	2

TABLE XXVI

CLASSIFIED INCOMES FOR THE YEARS 1903, 1904, 1906, AND 1907, FAMILY
OBLIGATIONS AND ORGANIZATION MEMBERSHIP OF CERTAIN WAGE-
EARNERS IN KANSAS— *Concluded*

Occupation.	Year.	Under $600.	$600 under $800.	$800 under $1,000.	$1,000 under $1,500.	$1,500 under $2,000.	$2,000 and over.	Total.	Number of heads of families.	Numbers *not* members of union.
Clerks	1903	14	7	2	2	....	....	25	13	......
"	1904	3	1	....	2	1	....	7	6	......
(Railroad)	1906	1	5	....	....	...	....	6	6	......
(Retail)	1907	....	5	....	....	...	....	5	3	(?) 5
Totals	....	18	18	2	4	1	....	43	28	(?) 5
Printers	1903	3	7	12	8	....	....	30	24	......
"	1904	4	11	11	12	2	....	40	28	......
"	1906	2	5	2	3	1	....	13	10	......
"	1907	2	10	11	3	....	....	26	19	......
Totals	....	11	33	36	26	3	....	109	81	......

These averages are purely abstract, but, on the whole, they
represent a group of incomes a little higher than at the beginning of the period, and a bit lower than at its close. Of
the Kansas workmen contributing, in the four years, these
1,574 replies, nearly thirty-six per cent, were earning less
than $600 per annum, thirty-two per cent received wages
amounting to $600 but less than $800, seventeen per cent
$800 and under $1,000, thirteen per cent $1,000 but less
than $1,500, and two per cent $1,500 or more. They were
mature men, members of unions. Owing largely to the
preponderation of the railroad employees, but partly to the
character of the returns from all the occupations, the range
of earnings in Iowa is much higher. Although these figures
are interesting as showing the distribution of labor incomes
in these two commonwealths, for several reasons they must
not be considered typical of the nation or even of these

DISTRIBUTION OF WAGES

TABLE XXVII

CLASSIFIED EARNINGS OF CERTAIN WAGE-EARNERS IN IOWA, 1905, 1907, AND 1909

Occupation.	Year.	Under $600.	$600 under $800.	$800 under $1,000.	$1,000 under $1,500.	$1,500 under $2,000.	$2,000 or over.	Totals.
Cigarmakers	1905	5	6	. . .	. . .	. . .	. . .	11
"	1907	1	5	5	. . .	. . .	. . .	11
"	1909	5	6	2	1	. . .	. . .	14
Totals	. .	11	17	7	1	. . .	. . .	36
Telegraph operators . .	1905	14	42	9	1	. . .	. . .	66
" " .	1907	5	21	7	5	. . .	. . .	38
" " .	1909	4	23	10	9	. . .	. . .	46
Totals	. .	23	86	26	15	. . .	. . .	150
Miners (coal)	1907	12	4	3	. . .	. . .	. .	19
"	1909	19	15	4	. . .	. . .	. . .	38
Totals	. .	31	19	7	. . .	. . .	. .	57
Bricklayers	1907	4	6	3	2	. . .	. . .	15
"	1909	2	6	5	7	1	. . .	21
Totals	. .	6	12	8	9	1	. . .	36
Clerks (retail)	1907	5	10	1	. . .	. . .	. . .	16
"	1909	7	9	4	5	. . .	1	26
Totals	. .	12	19	5	5	. . .	1	42
Letter-carriers	1905	. .	. . .	13	1	. . .	. . .	14
"	1909	3	5	2	19	. . .	. . .	29
Totals	. .	3	5	15	20	. . .	. . .	43

TABLE XXVII

CLASSIFIED EARNINGS OF CERTAIN WAGE EARNERS IN IOWA, 1905, 1907, AND 1909
— *Concluded*

Occupation.	Year.	Under $600.	$600 under $800.	$800 under $1,000.	$1,000 under $1,500.	$1,500 under $2,000.	$2,000 or over.	Totals.
Brakemen	1905	3	9	9	2	. .	. .	23
" (trainmen)	1907	. .	. .	. .	. .	. .	. .	. .
"	1909	. .	3	6	4	. .	. .	13
Totals	. .	3	12	15	6	. .	. .	36
Conductors	1905	. .	. .	1	13	4	. .	18
"	1907	. .	. .	1	9	3	. .	13
"	1909	. .	. .	3	10	6	. .	19
Totals	. .	. .	. .	5	32	13	. .	50
Engineers	1905	2	3	14	16	. .	. .	35
"	1907	. .	. .	2	13	16	. .	31
"	1909	. .	. .	3	27	19	1	50
Totals	. .	2	3	19	56	35	1	116
Firemen	1905	4	8	5	. .	. .	. .	17
"	1907	1	. .	2	5	. .	. .	8
"	1909	. .	2	5	7	. .	. .	14
Totals	. .	5	10	12	12	. .	. .	39
Trainmen	1905	3	10	8	1	. .	. .	22
"	1907	. .	2	7	. .	. .	. .	9
"	1909	. .	. .	. .	. .	. .	. .	. .
Totals	. .	3	12	15	1	. .	. .	31
Carpenters	1905	3	7	4	. .	. .	. .	14
"	1907	6	7	3	. .	. .	. .	16
"	1909	4	18	9	2	1	1	35
Totals	. .	13	32	16	2	1	1	65

TABLE XXVIII

SUMMARY TABLE OF CLASSIFIED INCOMES OF CERTAIN KANSAS WAGE-EARNERS, AND CLASSIFIED EARNINGS OF CERTAIN IOWA WAGE-EARNERS

	Numbers.							Percents.					
	Under $600.	$600 under $800.	$800 under $1,000.	$1,000 under $1,500.	$1,500 under $2,000.	$2,000 and over.	Totals.	Under $600.	$600 under $800.	$800 under $1,000.	$1,000 under $1,500.	$1,500 under $2,000.	$2,000 and over.
Kansas—													
Brakemen	4	11	18	2	....	....	35	12	31	51	6	....	....
Conductors	....	1	3	55	10	....	69	....	1	4	80	15	....
Engineers	1	3	....	28	15	2	49	2	6	....	57	31	4
Firemen	4	8	19	5	....	....	36	11	22	53	14	....	....
Carmen	31	45	13	1	....	....	90	35	50	14	1	....	....
Machinists	6	6	18	17	...	....	47	13	13	38	36	....	....
Other railroad employees	22	25	41	39	....	....	118	19	21	35	25	....	....
Brick and stone masons	31	28	21	17	3	....	100	31	28	21	17	3	....
Carpenters	96	127	42	8	....	....	273	35	47	15	3	....	....
Painters and paperhangers	18	19	7	1	....	....	45	40	42	16	2	....	....
Barbers	5	55	9	2	....	....	71	7	77	13	3	....	...
Cigarmakers	34	23	5	....	....	....	62	55	37	8	...	...	...
Miners and miner employees	143	68	26	3	....	....	240	60	28	11	1	....	....
Common laborers	78	16	3	....	....	....	97	80	17	3	....	....	....
Teamsters	63	23	2	2	....	....	90	70	26	2	2	....	....
Clerks	18	18	2	4	1	....	43	42	42	5	9	2	....
Printers	11	33	36	26	3	....	109	10	30	33	24	3	....
Totals	565	509	265	201	32	2	1574	35.9	32.4	16.8	12.8	2.0	.1
Iowa—													
Brakemen	3	12	15	6	....	....	36	8	33	42	17	....	....
Conductors	....	....	5	32	13	...	50	....	....	10	64	26	....
Engineers	2	3	19	56	35	1	116	2	3	16	48	30	1
Firemen	5	10	12	12	....	....	39	13	25	31	31	....	....
Trainmen	3	12	15	1	...	....	31	10	39	48	3	....	....
Carpenters	13	32	16	2	1	1	65	20	50	25	3	1	1
Cigarmakers	11	17	7	1	....	....	36	31	47	19	3	....	....
Telegraph operators	23	86	26	15	....	....	150	15	58	17	10	....	....
Bricklayers	6	12	8	9	1	....	36	17	33	22	25	3	....
Clerks	12	19	5	5	....	1	42	29	45	12	12	....	2
Letter carriers	3	5	15	20	....	....	43	7	11	35	47	....	...
Miners (coal)	31	19	7	....	....	....	57	55	33	12	....	....	....
Totals	112	227	150	159	50	3	701	16	32.4	21.4	22.7	7.1	.4

states. First, the Kansas returns, being almost exclusively from union men, have no determinable relation to the condition of the unorganized workers. Second, it is probably the more intelligent and the better-paid laborers who reply to such questionnaires as these states have circulated. Third, the cases are too few for any one year and occupation to be

trustworthy as a basis of generalization.[1] Fourth, the figures for Iowa are surprisingly at variance with the results
both of the 1905 *Census of Manufactures* and of the study
by the federal Labor Bureau in 1901, both of which show
for that state average earnings considerably lower than
those for the nation as a whole.[2] These tables, therefore,
depict wages too high to be considered quite representative.

While not, at first blush, as desirable as compilations of
annual compensation, the statistics of quarterly earnings
of the members of labor organizations, published by New
York State, by virtue of the fact that they automatically
make allowance for unemployment, are far preferable to
any of the other regularly available data. During the year,
there is variation from season to season, the building
trades, for example, being burdened by idleness to a greater
extent in the first three months than in the third, this phe-
nomenon manifests itself in the regularity with which the
average pay for the third quarter exceeds that for the first,
except when such unusual happenings as the famous Cloth-
ing Strike in the fall of 1910 interrupt the ordinary course
of events. Nevertheless, within bounds, these New York
returns can be considered a fair indication of the distribution of annual earnings among the union workingmen of
the Empire State.

---

[1] Not all the replies received by these states in the years under discussion have been used in making the summaries. Many occupations
were represented in but one year, or by less than five persons in each
year. These have been omitted, as a class entitled "miscellaneous"
would not represent the same group of crafts from year to year.

[2] *Census of Manufactures*, 1905, pt. iv, p. 670, shows average weekly
earnings of males sixteen years and over in factories to be $11.16
for nation and $10.48 for Iowa, which ranked thirty-fourth among the
states for average earnings of men, p. 672. *Eighteenth Annual Report
of the Commissioner of Labor*, p. 366, shows annual earnings of heads
of families to have averaged $621 for the United States, $511 for Iowa.

TABLE XXIX [1]

QUARTERLY EARNINGS OF ORGANIZED WORKINGMEN IN NEW YORK STATE

	First quarter							Third quarter						
	Per cent earning				Average earnings	Index number		Per cent earning				Average earnings	Index number	
Year	Less than $75	$150–$225 below				Daily wages	Quarters' earnings	Less than $75					Daily wages	Quarters' earnings
I.	II. Less than $75	III. $75–$149	IV. $150–$225	V. Over $225	VI.	VII. Daily wages	VIII. Quarters' earnings	IX. Less than $75	X. $75–$149	XI. $150–$225	XII. Over $225	XIII.	XIV. Daily wages	XV. Quarters' earnings
1897	5.7	28.7	45.4	20.2	$145	98	98	....	....	....	....	$174	96	94
1898	6.1	29.1	41.9	22.9	164	98	96	....	....	....	....	175	97	91
1899	6.5	26.6	41.1	25.8	172	99	97	2.5	22.1	41.9	33.5	197	99	102
1900	3.8	27.0	41.8	27.4	176	101	100	4.5	34.0	47.1	14.4	182	100	95
1901	3.9	23.3	46.7	26.1	183	101	103	2.3	22.6	42.9	32.2	194	101	103
1902	7.5	27.4	41.7	23.8	184	102	105	1.6	24.0	43.0	31.4	197	104	106
1903	8.9	21.0	43.3	26.8	186	108	110	3.1	23.7	43.9	29.3	190	108	107
1904	2.2	18.8	40.6	38.4	176	110	106	4.2	22.5	42.0	31.3	196	111	110
1905	2.9	20.0	39.9	37.2	187	114	114	2.5	15.7	41.1	41.9	219	114	117
1906	6.0	24.1	35.5	34.4	212	116	126	1.3	12.9	39.5	46.3	225	117	120
1907	3.6	20.8	38.2	37.4	205	119	122	0.9	14.0	40.8	44.3	227	118	122
1908	3.8	17.2	38.8	40.1	200	120	114	3.3	21.9	37.4	37.4	207	118	109
1909	2.8	21.8	33.2	42.2	209	120	118	1.1	11.9	37.0	50.0	233	121	121
1910	1.9	20.1	39.4	38.6	214	123	124	3.4	22.5	30.8	43.3	213	124	124
1911					213	125	123	2.2	14.9	33.6	49.3	226	125	123
1912					210	128	127							

[1] New York, *Annual Report of the Bureau of Labor Statistics*, 1904, pp. liii and lv; 1908, pp. xxvii, xxx. *Bulletin, Department of Labor*, no. 47, pp. 211, 212, 213; no. 46, pp. 17, 19, 20; no. 49, pp. 480, 481; no. 51, pp. 109, 110.

Table XXIX would seem to indicate that, both in average and in distribution, the compensation of union workingmen in New York is tending on the whole to improve.[1] That, with one exception, for each of the last six quarters on record, more than forty per cent of these men have earned at least $225, does not necessarily lead to the conclusion that over forty per cent are receiving as much as $900 per annum nor does it inevitably follow from the table that, as a rule, the remuneration of between twenty and twenty-five per cent falls below $600 a year: the income of each individual is more or less subject to fluctuation, he may be in one group this season, and in another the next. Neither must these figures be interpreted as applicable to the entire laboring force of New York State, for they relate only to union men. If, however, one assumes that employers consistently seek, in time of business dullness, to lay off the more inefficient hands first, then it is not unreasonable to hold that forty per cent or more of the organized male workers in New York enjoy incomes of at least $900, and that well up toward twenty-five per cent do not earn as much as $600.

The fact that a large proportion of the men employed in the telephone business possess, of necessity, more or less skill arouses the expectation that their wages are rather higher than those in most industrial occupations. Table XXX shows this to be the case. Judging by their monthly pay, seventeen per cent of these men receive less than $600 per year, about fifty-six per cent earn $600 but under $960, and the remaining twenty-seven per cent get $960 or more, three per cent enjoying at least $1,500. These figures cover practically the entire public telephone industry in the United States, and include all males employed, no criterion of their ages being furnished.

[1] *Money earnings,* conf., p. 274, note.

TABLE XXX[1]

MONTHLY RATES OF WAGES OF MALES IN THE TELEPHONE INDUSTRY, FOR A PAY
ROLL PERIOD IN 1908

I.	II.	III.
Monthly rate of pay.	Number of males.	Per cent.
Under $25	336	2.15
$25 but under $50........	2,333	14.99
50 " " 60........	2,782	17.90
60 " " 70........	2,970	19.09
70 " " 80........	3,011	19.33
80 " " 90........	1,385	8.91
90 " " 100........	1,325	8.51
100 " " 125........	909	5.84
125 and over............	512	3.28
Totals	15,563	100.00

In 1902, it will be remembered, the Census Bureau investigated *Central Electric Light and Power Stations*. In the
report were published the classified wages of 18,878 of the
employees, presumably all men. Since at that time the industry maintained, altogether, some twenty-six thousand
wage earners, the sample was probably quite representative.[2]
Of these men, nearly 46 per cent were given less than $2.00
per diem or a maximum of $626 for the year, unless they
were employed seven days to the week; about as many more
were paid $2.00 but less than $3.00, leaving but eight per
cent to be remunerated with three dollars or more, the full
time equivalent of from nine to eleven hundred dollars a
year, depending on the number of holidays and Sundays not
worked.

[1] *Investigation of the Telephone Companies*, pp. 294, 298, 300, compiled.

[2] *Special Census Report on Central Electric Light and Power Stations*, pp. 116, 117, 132, 133.

TABLE XXXI[1]

WAGES OF EMPLOYEES OF CENTRAL ELECTRIC LIGHT AND POWER STATIONS, 1902

I.	II.	III.
Daily wages.	Men.	Per cent.
Under $1.................	362	1.9
$1.00–$1.24..............	990	5.2
1.25– 1.49	1,613	8.5
1.50– 1.74.............	3,380	17.9
1.75– 1.99.............	2,314	12.3
2.00– 2.24.........	4,089	21.7
2.25– 2.49.............	1,807	9.6
2.50– 2.74.....	1,899	10.1
2.75– 2.99.............	823	4.4
3.00– 3.24	832	4.4
3.25– 3.49.............	309	1.6
3.50– 3.74.............	191	1.0
3.75 and over	269	1.4
Totals	18,878	100.0

In the same year, 1902, the Census Bureau investigated
also the *Mines and Quarries* of the United States and published a table showing the classified wages of the 581,728
male employees of all the incorporated companies. Among
these wage earners were some 11,857 boys under sixteen
years of age. Of all males occupied in the mines and
quarries, 42.8 per cent were receiving less than $2.00 per
day, 45 per cent $2.00 but less than $3.00, and the remaining 12.2 per cent $3.00 or more. Of the anthracite coal
miners, 62.7 per cent were paid at a per diem rate less
than $2.00, and 84.8 per cent less than $2.50; in the bituminous mines the corresponding percents were respectively
33.0 and 73.8. Unemployment is such a large factor in

[1] *Special Census Report, Central Electric Light and Power Station,*
p. 60; the figures cover all wage-earners save those classed as miscellaneous occupations in 80 per cent of the plants.

curtailing the earning power of coal miners that it would be unsafe to base any estimate of annual compensation upon these daily wages. According to the figures in Tables XXV and XXVIII, over 81 per cent of the coal miners in the country were receiving, in 1901, less than $600 per annum, in Kansas, about 1905, 60 per cent. The fact that the great Anthracite Coal Strike of 1904 and the joint agreements have probably raised the rates of pay above those shown in Table XXXII, is another reason for refusing to build much upon this report.

TABLE XXXII [1]

DAILY WAGES OF THE EMPLOYEES OF INCORPORATED COMPANIES, MINES AND QUARRIES IN 1902

I.	II.	III.	IV.
	Per cents.		
Daily wages (rate).	All minerals.	Anthracite coal.	Bituminous coal.
Less than $1	2.8	9.1	1.4
$1.00 –1.49....................	13.6	21.6	7.1
1.50– 1.99....................	26.4	32.0	24.5
2.00– 2.49....................	31.7	22.1	40.8
2.50– 2.99....................	13.3	7.1	17.2
3.00– 3.49....................	7.2	4.6	6.6
3.50– 3.99....................	3.9	2.6	2.1
4.00 and over	1.1	.9	.3
Number of men	581,728	69,691	280,638

The statistics of distribution of wages and earnings so far presented have been drawn mainly from the groups of manufacturing, transportation, and mining, but in the totals of the *Eighteenth Annual Report of the Commis-*

[1] *Census, Mines and Quarries,* 1902, p. 96.

sioner of Labor,[1] were included some returns from the branches of industry known as trade, and domestic and personal service; moreover, data from a few agricultural laborers were given place. Although there seems to be no recent and extensive government study of the earnings of professional men, some information is available. In the first place, the salaries of school teachers in cities having a population of 8,000 or more have been classified under the direction of the late Carroll D. Wright for the National Education Association. Some of the results of this work have been compressed into the following table:

TABLE XXXIII [2]

SALARIES OF MALE TEACHERS IN PUBLIC SCHOOLS IN CITIES OF 8,000 OR OVER, 1905

I.	II.	III.	IV.
		Per cents.	
Salary.	High school teachers.	Elementary school.	
		Principals.	Teachers.
Under $600.....................	2.15	4.26	19.31
$600 under 800	12.84	10.67	13.20
800 " 1,000	15.28	14.18	12.26
1,000 " 1,200	17.95	10.13	12.47
1,200 " 1,500	19.66	15.22	17.09
1,500 " 2,000	18.79	20.73	25.67
2,000 and over..................	13.33	24.81	....
Totals	100.00	100.00	100.00
Number.	2,874	2,378	1,492
Average salary.	$1303	$1542	$1161

[1] Tables XXIV and XXV.

[2] *Report on Salaries, Tenure and Pensions of Public School Teachers in the United States,* pp. 17-22.

While this summary is doubtless accurate enough, it by no means represents the earnings of all male teachers in the United States; a glance at the reports of the Commissioner of Education will convince any one that the masters of district schools receive very low wages. Further, since the Census does not furnish the numbers of secondary school instructors and of elementary principals and teachers in the United States, it is impossible to know the sizes of the groups represented by these figures of salary distribution. It is, however, a surprising fact that only 13.33 per cent of the high-school teachers, a large proportion of whom are presumably well-educated men, are drawing salaries of $2,000 or more.

The *Census of Religious Bodies,* 1906, shows the average salary of ministers of all denominations to have been $663, but gives no idea of the distribution of these remunerations.[1] The mean for the Methodist Episcopal Church was $812, considerably above the general average. The various Conferences of this denomination publish *Annual Minutes* in which are recorded the salary of each minister and, if the church owns such a building, the rental value of the parsonage. The 1910 minutes of ten fairly typical conferences were selected, and the incomes of the 1,504 connected ministers noted. Including the worth of these parsonages, the annual remuneration of 30.9 per cent of these men was less than $600, of 34.6 per cent $600 but under $1,000; 78.7 per cent of them received less than $1,200, and but 4.6 per cent, as much as $2,000. In view of the fact that the mean pay of the Methodist ministers was found by the Census to be over twenty per cent higher than the average compensation of all clergymen, in Table XXXIV is exhibited a better distribution of incomes than would be found among the entire 108,000 members of this profession.

[1] Vol. i, pp. 94-97.

TABLE XXXIV

INCOMES OF 1504 METHODIST EPISCOPAL MINISTERS IN 1910

(Salary plus rental value of parsonage)

I.	II.	III.
Income.	Number.	Per cent.
Under $600..............................	464	30.9
$ 600 under $800	275	18.3
800 " 1,000	245	16.3
1,000 " 1,200	199	13.2
1,200 " 1,500	150	10.0
1,500 " 2,000	102	6.7
2,000 " 2,500	44	2.9
2,500 " 3,000	13	.9
3,000 " 4,000	10	.7
4,000 and over	2	.1
Totals	1504	100.0

One great field of endeavor remains untouched.[1] True, Table XXV shows the classified annual earnings of agricultural laborers, but it throws no light upon the incomes of the five million, seven hundred thousand farm families. This lack is partially relieved by the *Census of Agriculture* which classifies farms according to the value of their products not fed to live stock.

[1] There are no reliable statistics of the incomes of physicians, but Dr. Taylor, of Philadelphia, estimated that 100,000 of them "average $1,000 a year; 20,000, $2,000 per annum; 8,000, $3,000; 5,000, $5,000; 1,500, $10,000; 200, $20,000; 150, $25,000; 100, $30,000; and 50 physicians average $45,000 a year." " Dr. Shrady, of New York, places the annual average income of 100,000 physicians at from $800 to $1,000. He says that two or three physicians in New York make over $100,000 each year; five or six range from $50,000 to $60,000, fifty from $25,000 to $30,000." Editorial, *The American Medical Compend*, March, 1904, vol. xx, no. 3, p. 76.

TABLE XXXV [1]

FARMS CLASSIFIED BY THE VALUE OF PRODUCTS NOT FED TO LIVE STOCK, 1899

I.		II.	III.
Value of products not fed to live stock.		Number of farms.	Per cent.
. . . .		53,406	.9
$1 but under	$50.	167,569	2.9
50 "	100.	305,590	5.3
100 "	250.	1,247,731	21.8
250 "	500.	1,602,854	27.9
500 "	1,000.	1,378,944	24.0
1,000 "	2,500.	829,443	14.5
2,500 and over	. . . .	154,120	2.7
		5,739,657	100.0

As has been pointed out, the exact distribution of incomes among farm families is not revealed by these figures, for the following reasons: first, in reckoning the value of the products of each farm, no allowance was made for purchases of feed, seed, and fertilizer; second, no deduction was made for rent; third, the wages paid to hired help were not accounted for; fourth, subsidiary incomes, either from rent of another farm owned by the proprietor of the place in question, or from other investments, or from labor performed outside, were not considered; fifth, as ideas on the cost of living in the country are even more vague than those as to the minimum of subsistence in cities, the welfare of these farm families cannot be compared with that of industrial households. What allowance should be made for errors from these opposing sources, it is impossible to say. However, that for a year when all crops except cotton were normal, the Census should show the total value of the products of 30.9 per cent of the farms to be under $250, and of

[1] *Twelfth Census*, vol. v, *Agriculture*, pt. i, pp. lxiv, lx.

58.8 per cent to be less than $500, is a safe indication that so far as money is a criterion, farming is not much, if any, more profitable than ordinary urban labor.[1]

The distribution of earnings among federal civil-service employees is shown in the following table. It is immediately patent that the government is a model employer.

TABLE XXXVI[2]

DISTRIBUTION OF COMPENSATION OF EMPLOYEES IN EXECUTIVE CIVIL SERVICE, 1907

I.	II.	III.
	Males.	
Earnings group.	Number.	Per cent.
Less than $720	28,812	16.7
$ 720 less than $840	20,331	11.8
840 " " 900	10,299	6.0
900 " " 1,000	42,486	24.7
1,000 " " 1,200	32,696	19.0
1,200 " " 1,400	16,814	9.8
1,400 " " 1,600	8,760	5.1
1,600 " " 1,800	3,186	1.9
1,800 " " 2,000	2,911	1.7
2,000 " " 2,500	2,305	1.3
2,500 and over	1,872	1.1
Piece work	1,136	.7
Without pay	16	..
Not reported.............................	429	.2
	172,053	100.0

[1] The large percents in the low-product groups cannot be entirely explained away by the errors which may have been incurred through the cropping system and similar schemes for cultivation in the South. For instance, a dozen small farms tilled by negroes may have been entered as having a valueless product, but their total output may have been listed as that of a farm (plantation) producing a crop (cotton?) worth over $2,500. (But there is a considerable percentage of farms

The present chapter has attained such proportions that it may be well to summarize the conclusions.

1. Between four and five-tenths of the industrial families of the United States are entirely supported by the earnings of the father-husband, and the probability of a supplementary income is decreased, up to a certain unknown point, with every increase of the wages of the head of the household.

2. Wages in the factories of New York are vastly higher than at the close of the Civil War when measured by purchasing power, but very little higher in money.

3. Although state statistics show a tendency for money earnings to rise in recent years, an increase in real wages, as measured in terms of purchasing power of food, is doubtful. The *Dewey Report* and the 1905 *Census of Manufactures* show a probable decline in the average wages in this important branch of industry between 1890 and 1904. Between 1890 and 1900, the distribution of wages about the mean became distinctly less satisfactory, but in the years 1900 to 1904 there seems to have been a slight reversal of this tendency.

4. Since 1904 the state figures indicate an improvement of the money wages of men in factories. The extent of this improvement for the nation at large cannot be ascertained.

in each of the sections of the country, and also in the hands of each race, in the low-products group.) See *Twelfth Census*, vol. v, *Agriculture*, pt. i, pp. lx, lxx; also *Abstract*, pp. 222, 233.

² *Bulletin of the Twelfth Census*, No. 94, *Statistics of Employees, Executive Civil Service of the United States*, p. 20. The persons referred to in this bulletin as "employees in the executive Civil Service" include practically all of the employees in the Civil Service of the United States with the exception of persons in the consular and diplomatic service, the postmasters, the clerks in postoffices not having free delivery, the mechanics and laborers in navy yards and naval stations, and the employees of the Isthmian Canal Commission employed on the Isthmus.

5. The *Census of Manufactures* showed that, in 1904, 62.1 per cent of the males, sixteen years of age or over, employed in factories were earning less than $12 per week, the equivalent (full time) of $626 or less annually. Six per cent were paid $20 or more weekly, $1,043 or more per year, full time.

6. The earnings of heads of families range higher than those of all males who have passed their sixteenth birthday.

7. In 1901, 47.56 per cent of the heads of industrial families, having an income less than $1,200 per annum, earned less than $600; 34.71 per cent received $600 and less than $800; 5.40 per cent, $1,000 or over. $1,200 seems to be almost the limit of wage earnings in most industrial occupations.

8. From 1903 to 1907, in Kansas, about thirty-six per cent of mature organized workingmen received less than $600, thirty-two per cent $600 but less than $800, fifteen per cent over $1,000.

9. In New York, in recent years, between seventeen and twenty-five per cent of the organized workingmen have earned less than $150 per quarter, and over forty per cent have received $225 or more.

10. About seventeen per cent of the males in the telephone industry are paid under $600 a year, fifty-six per cent $600 but under $960, nine per cent $1,200 or over.

11. Nearly forty-six per cent of the men employed in central electric light and power stations, in 1902, were paid less than $2.00 per day, and nearly another forty-six per cent $2.00 but less than $3.00.

12. In the mines and quarries, in 1902, 42.8 per cent of the males employed earned less than $2.00 daily, 45.0 per cent $2.00 but less than $3.00. Among these males, however, were 11,857 boys under sixteen years of age (two per cent of all).

13. Male teachers in cities of at least 8,000 population receive salaries much above the wages in industry, over ninety per cent earning at least $600, and nearly seventy per cent at least $1,000.

14. Of Methodist Episcopal ministers, better paid than the average of all denominations, 30.9 per cent have incomes under $600 per annum; 34.6 per cent, $600 but under $1,000; 4.6 per cent, $2,000 or over.

15. According to the Census of Agriculture, in 1899, on 58.8 per cent of the farms of the United States the total value of all products not fed to live stock was under $500; on 24 per cent the value was $500 but under $1,000.

16. The United States government is more liberal with its compensation of ordinary labor than private employers.

The validity of any sweeping generalization which might be based upon these sixteen statements, would be subject to doubt. It is, however, desirable to describe the distribution of earnings among the largest possible group of men. The obtaining of this description involves an estimate. Estimates are at best only approximations of the truth, but they may, nevertheless, serve useful purposes. It is, however, *essential* to science that the real character of an estimate be appreciated; it is a guess, presumably a " wise guess ", based upon a thorough consideration of the known facts, and subject to alteration as soon as new and better information is presented.

With this caution, it is not improper to submit the following estimate of the distribution of money earnings, first among the industrial people, that is, among males of at least sixteen years engaged in manufacturing, mining, and in some branches of trade, transportation, and personal service; and, second, among these industrial workers combined with ministers, agricultural laborers, and farm families. In the table, the third column gives the approximate number of males sixteen years of age or over engaged in 1904 in the occupation or industry named in column I. The rest of the table was constructed as follows: taking " barbers and hair dressers ", for example, the " a " in column II signifies that, on the whole, the best statistics covering men in this trade are to be found in Table XXV of this essay, which shows that about forty-two per cent of the barbers investigated in 1901 earned less than $600, about fifty-seven per cent $600 but less than $1,000, and less than one per cent, $1,000 or over. Using these proportions and re-cording the results in round numbers, columns IV, V, and VI were filled in—forty-two per cent of 134,000 being 56,280, for instance. The men engaged in manufacture could not be treated in exactly this way, as annual com-pensations are not available; the number of these persons earning less than $12 per week was placed in column IV, the number receiving $12 but less than $20 in column V, and the number paid $20 or over in column VI. The same process was used in distributing the " miners and quarry-men—not coal ", except that, from the total number of miners and quarrymen, belonging in each column accord-ing to the census, was subtracted the number of coal miners in that column, approximately according to the Kansas dis-tribution; thus the Census group of 582,000 was divided into two classes. The cost of living being lower outside than within cities, the number of agricultural laborers earn-ing less than $400 was placed in column IV, along with the number of farm families, or more strictly speaking, of *farms,* the products of which were valued at less than $500. Corresponding changes were made in column V. With this explanation, the table should be intelligible.

TABLE XXXVII

ESTIMATE OF THE DISTRIBUTION OF INCOMES PRIMARILY FROM LABOR

I. Occupation or industry.	II. Basis of estimate.	III. Approximate number of males, 16 years old or over, employed in 1904.	IV. Number earning under $600 yearly, or under $12 weekly.	V. Number earning $600, but under $1,000 yearly, $12 but under $20 weekly.	VI. Number earning $1,000 or more yearly, or $20 or more weekly.
Barbers and hairdressers	a.	134,000	56,000	77,000	1,000
Bartenders	a.	95,000	29,000	65,000	1,000
Janitors and sextons	a.	52,000	31,000	20,000	1,000
Laborers domestic and personal)	a.	2,691,000	2,516,000	175,000	....
Draymen, hac men, teamsters...............	a.	568,000	360,000	208,000	....
Steam railroad, firemen....................	b.	55,000	6,000	41,000	8,000
Enginemen	b.	52,000	1,000	3,000	48,000
Conductors	b.	40,000	....	2,000	38,000
Machinists	b.	46,000	6,000	24,000	16,000
Other trainmen (brakemen)........	b.	107,000	13,000	88,000	6,000
Switch tenders, etc................	c.	46,000	18,000	23,000	5,000
Other trackmen (section hands)....	a.	289,000	245,000	44,000	....
Clerks and copyists	c.	569,000	132,000	323,000	114,000
Carpenters and joiners	b.	645,000	226,000	400,000	19,000
Masons (brick and stone)	b.	173,000	53,000	85,000	35,000
Painters, glaziers, varnishers	a.	294,000	127,000	161,000	6,000
Miners and quarrymen, coal................	b.	351,000	210,000	137,000	4,000
Not coal....................	b. & d.	231,000	38,000	167,000	26,000
Manufactures.....	e.	4,245,000	2,664,000	1,325,000	256,000
Totals, industrial	......	10,683,000	6,731,000	3,368,000	584,000
Ministers	g.	106,000	33,000	36,000	37,000
Agricultural laborers	a. y.	3,129,000	2,597,000	532,000	....
Farm families	f. x.	5,740,000	3,377,000	1,379,000	984,000
Totals.............................	......	19,658,000	12,738,000	5,315,000	1,605,000

[1]The bases of the estimate are as follows:

a. *Eighteenth Annual Report of the Commissioner of Labor,* or in this essay, Table XXV.

b. Reports of the Kansas Bureau of Labor, or Table XXVIII.

c. Slight modification of the proportions in " a."

d. *Census of Mines and Quarries*—includes 11,800 boys under sixteen years of age, Table XXXII.

e. *Census of Manufactures,* 1905, Table XXI.

f. *Census of Agriculture,* 1900, Table XXXV.

g. Table XXXIV.

x. In column iv are placed all farms the value of whose products,

The reason for including in column III the approximate number of men employed in each branch of work in 1904, is the fact that at present the largest compilation of classified wage data is the Census of Manufactures for that year; the statistics showing earnings in other occupations relate to years on both sides of 1904. Doubtless it is inaccurate to combine figures for different dates, yet it has already been noted that the rise of compensation in manufactures between 1900 and 1904 was very slight, if it was not entirely imaginary; there is, moreover, no evidence of a considerable advance in other wages during this period. Consequently, it is probable that, including in the same table results of computations based on studies made in different years entails, in this case, no great error.

It requires little ingenuity to find faults in this summary table. For instance, among the " farm families " the Census enumerated about three hundred thousand establishments headed by women; the bases of some of the estimates

not fed to live-stock, was less than $500; in column v the number of farms producing to the value of $500, but less than $1,000; in column vi the number producing $1,000 or more.

y. In column iv is placed the number earning less than $400; in column v those earning $400 but less than $1,000. This is done that the difference in cost of living in urban and rural localities may be somewhat taken into account in a rough way.

As only 100 agricultural laborers were included in the Bureau of Labor investigation, the basis for the distribution of the earnings of three million men may seem absurdly small. However, the average earnings of the 100 was $269. An investigation of the Michigan Bureau of Labor in 1905, covering 5,922 farms in 1,210 towns, showed that farm hands worked an average of 8.5 months at a mean wage, including value of board, of $23.11, or $196 per year. (*Michigan, Report Bureau of Labor*, 1905, p. 347.) Doubtless there are many localities in the North where the earnings of agricultural labor are greater than this, but there are other communities where help, especially in the South, gets much less. So probably the distribution shown in the Bureau of Labor Report is substantially correct.

are narrow; there is not an exact coincidence in the nomen-
clature of occupations between the various sources of statistics; the year 1904 is long past; there is such a combination of wages and annual earnings in the data that there
can be no strict line between the income groups; it is impossible to determine the distribution of yearly remuneration from that of weekly pay. On the other hand, except
in the cases of manufacturing and mining, the estimate is
based on the compensation of mature men—mostly heads
of families, and, in some trades, members of labor unions;
moreover, where wage statistics were used, it was impossible to make any legitimate allowance for unemployment.
Most of these inaccuracies would tend to make the distribution of annual earnings, among males sixteen years or more
of age, appear better than, in 1904, it actually was.

In view of this consideration, and of the general harmony
of the statistics presented in this chapter, it is reasonable to
believe that, in 1904, something over sixty per cent of the
males at least sixteen years of age, employed in manufacturing, mining, trade, transportation, and a few other
occupations associated with industrial life, were earning
less than $626 per annum, about thirty per cent were re-
ceiving $626 but under $1,044, and perhaps ten per cent enjoyed labor incomes of at least $1,000. If to these the agri-
culturists are added, sixty-five per cent fall in the low-
earnings group, twenty-seven in the medium, and eight in
the high. Suppose all the men engaged in gainful occupations in 1904, but unaccounted for in this estimate, to
have been paid $12 per week or more. This is manifestly
impossible, yet, even upon such an assumption, fully one-
half of the adult males engaged in remunerative labor were
rewarded that year with less than $626.

CHAPTER VII

INCOMES FROM PROPERTY

IN 1900 the Census Bureau estimated the value of the total wealth of the United States at about eighty-eight and a half billion dollars, and in 1904 at just over one hundred seven billion. If, since that time, this rate of increase has been consistently maintained the riches of the nation were close to one hundred forty-three billion in 1910 and to one hundred fifty-six billion in 1912. A large proportion of this wealth is productive, for instance, the farm lands,[1] mines, quarries, factories, railways, telephones, telegraphs, and other forms of business property, and a large part of the residential real estate. Desirable as it would be to know the distribution of this income-yielding property, it is, as appeared in Chapter III, impossible even to approximate the number of individuals who possess it. There are, however, some hints as to the extent of ownership, which are well worth consideration.

On June 7, 1911, the 1,884 savings banks in the United States had 9,597,185 accounts, aggregating $4,212,583,598, an average of $438.93.[2] It is a perfectly well-known fact that the number of individual depositors is less than the number of accounts, as well-to-do persons frequently have money in several institutions at the same time. On the other hand, one acquainted with such large savings banks

[1] The advance figures of the census of 1910 show an increase in value of farm lands from $13,058,008,000 in 1900 to $28,386,770,000 in 1910.

[2] *American Year-Book for 1911*, p. 303.

as the Bowery, the Dime of Brooklyn, or the Williams-
burgh, can confidently assert that the great mass of bene-
ficiaries are working people.   Thursday afternoon, for instance, is sometimes known as " Servant Girls' Day ".   In
1910, there were eighty-seven savings banks in Connecticut
with 575,913 depositors, of whom 492,773, or 85.5 per cent,
had balances of under $1,000 each; not less than $1,000 but
less than $2,000 was due to 54,669 persons, or 9.5 per cent;
$2,000 or more, to 28,741 individuals or five per cent of
the depositors.   This five per cent had total claims amounting to $101,544,660, the first eighty-five and a half per cent
to $101,682,710, the average of all accounts being $478.96.[1]
In the fiscal year ending June 30, 1910, the mutual savings
banks in the United States paid their customers dividends
averaging 3.92 per cent, the mean return in the stock savings banks was 3.56 per cent.[2]   Some depositors make a
practice of regularly drawing their " interest ".   It is thus
apparent that, whatever allowance must be made for duplications among the owners of the nine and a half-million
accounts, there is a large number of people, mostly of small
means, who are regularly deriving some income from savings banks.   The dividends due one individual may seldom
be large, but they aggregate over $110,000,000 per annum.

Another form of saving is life insurance.   Although the
twenty-three million odd industrial policies are a form of
thrift, they are not properly income-yielding investments,
at least in the sense, that dividends do not accrue to their

[1] *Report of the Bank Commissioners, State of Connecticut, for year
ending Sept. 30, 1910*, p. 11.

[2] It should be noted that dividends are paid only on money actually
in the bank on the dividend day, having been on deposit at least three
months.   Savings banks do not pay "interest on daily balances."   In
mutual savings banks all the earnings belong to the depositors.   Stock
savings banks are run for profit by corporations, which appropriate
part of the earnings.   *Conf.*   Table XXXIX.

owners. However, nearly seventy-three per cent of the $13,227,213,168 of ordinary insurance carried, on some 6,-954,119 policies, is "participating". In 1910, the dividends paid to the holders of these policies amounted to $75,353,638. Needless to say cash was not often directly given to the insured, but the amount of the profit was either deducted from the necessary premium, reserved against future obligations, or added to the value of the policy. Thus whatever of this sum was actually deducted from payments or used to increase principal is the equivalent of income to the policy holder. Insurance is therefore another form of property which yields a real, if individually small, income to literally millions of persons.[1]

Nearly as widely distributed as savings accounts and insurance policies is productive real estate. In 1910, there were some 6,340,357 farms of which 2,622,341 were owned outright by the families that tilled them; another 1,311,364 mortgaged farms were occupied by the title holders; 2,349,254 were worked by tenants and 57,398 by managers.[2] How much of the $8,926,000,000 gross agricultural products were imputable to the land and capital, and how much to the labor of the farmers and their help cannot be determined from the existing data. It is clear, however, that at least 3,933,705 persons, probably well up toward five million owned agricultural property, and since the value of these farms more than doubled in a decade, it is safe to conclude that the large majority receive incomes properly attributable to this real estate.

The 1910 figures for residential real estate are not yet published. As has been indicated, in 1900, nearly sixty-

[1] F. L. Hoffman, *Quarterly Publications of the American Statistical Association*, no. 95, vol. xii, Sept. 1911, pp. 684, 735, 748.

[2] *Advance Statement of the Thirteenth Census, General Data on Agriculture.*

four per cent of the families not on the farms hired their
tenements, and only 23.4 per cent owned their homes free
of encumbrance. Of those who did hold title to their dwellings certainly most enjoyed a psychic income, and many
an additional financial benefit, inasmuch as they did not
pay rent. Subtract upkeep and taxes from the cost of accommodations of the same grade, and what remains is the
income to the owner from his possession, nonetheless real
because he does not calculate it in money. On the other
hand, the 4,999,302 households hiring their quarters were,
at least in the greater part, contributing to the property income of their landlords, but the number of these proprietors and the amount of their revenue is hidden. Here
again is painfully apparent the impossibility of statistically
treating the distribution of property incomes.

Not a bit more satisfactory is the information relating
to the ownership of factories. Although the schedule of
the 1910 Census of Manufactures called for the number
of " proprietors and partnership members, if a non-incor-
porated organization ", and of stockholders, if a corporation, the returns so far published give only 273,265 as the
number of " proprietors and firm members " of the 268,491
establishments.[1] Even if the total of the numbers of stockholders in the separate establishments was known, because
of the infinite possibilities of duplications among the owners of the 69,501 incorporated plants, it would be as little
representative of the true state of affairs as the data on the
holders of railway and industrial securities discussed in
Chapter III. Since allowance for the proper depreciation
charges has been carefully avoided, and since no data is
offered regarding the interest on funded debts, the Bureau
of the Census is extremely careful to warn the world

---

[1] *Census Bulletin, Manufactures: United States,* p. 3.

against drawing any conclusions as to profits in manufacturing.

Further citation of " near-facts " would be profitless, but it may be worth while to mention the light which may be gained from the tax lists. In 1895, the New Jersey Bureau of Statistics of Labor and Industry published the following table:

TABLE XXXVIII [1]

DISTRIBUTION OF ASSESSMENTS IN NEWARK, CAMDEN, JERSEY CITY, AND PATTERSON
IN 1895

I.	II.	III.	IV.
Assessment.	Individuals.	Firms.	Corporations.
$1,000– $2,000	17,832	336	158
2,000– 3,000	11,033	220	116
3,000– 4,000	6,576	140	85
4,000– 5,000	3,838	82	73
5,000– 10,000	5,596	240	169
10,000– 15,000	1,316	97	97
15,000– 25,000	886	85	114
25,000– 50,000	440	72	105
50,000–100,000	163	36	85
100,000 and over	91	17	101
	47,771	1,325	1,103

The population of Newark, Camden, Jersey City, and Patterson, in 1895, was found to be 559,330; 8,492 individuals, or 1.5 per cent of the population, were believed, by the assessors, each to own at least $5,000 worth of real and personal property. These persons probably belonged to not more than eight per cent of the families. The 47,771 possessors of at least $1,000 worth of assessable property were 8.54 per cent of the population and could hardly have repre-

[1] *Report N. J. Bu. Stat. Lab. and Industry,* 1895, p. 169.

sented forty per cent of the families in the four municipalities.

New Britain, Connecticut, " the Hardware City ", is a typical cosmopolitan industrial center. Its " Grand List " for 1910 showed $37,002,903 of taxable property, of which $36,700,000 was invested in land, houses, stores and their stocks, mills and factories, and manufacturing and mechanical operations. In this city an effort has been made to rate all wealth at its full market price, but in spite of the stringent Connecticut oath personalty seems to escape. Assuming that residential real estate yields income. the distribution of taxed values will correspond closely with the diffusion of tangible productive property. Inspection of the Grand List shows that 988 individuals, 2.25 per cent of the population, were assessed for upwards of $5,000; 2,364 persons, 5.38 per cent of the inhabitants, for at least $2,000: and that 3,468 names were on the books as more than " polls ". Perhaps one-eighth of the families in the city were worth $5,000 or over, and one-third could command as much as an even thousand dollars.

These tax statistics from New Jersey and Connecticut are not cited as proof that approximately an eighth of the urban households of the United States are possessed of productive property to the value of $5,000. The point is. first, that the number of families deriving any considerable income from the direct ownership of tangible wealth is exceedingly small, and second, that, because of the obvious failure to reach many forms of capital, the general property tax can offer no safe ground for inference as to the distribution of incomes.[1]

In 1892 and 1902. the *Tribune* and the *World* published

---

[1] In New Britain not an individual reported money on hand or on deposit exceeding $100, or ownership of stock liable to taxation.

lists of American millionaires. On the first, there were 4,047 names and on the second 3,045;[1] but it is extremely difficult to believe that the number of such fortunes had actually decreased in the decade. The *Financial Red Book of America*, a volume apparently designed to facilitate soliciting, gives the names of over eighteen thousand " rich men ".

The endeavor to determine the number of persons or of families enjoying incomes from the ownership of property cannot at present lead to a definite result. There are probably nine million individuals receiving some return on savings accounts, and upward of five million indirectly obtaining profit from participating life-insurance policies. About five million persons possess agricultural land, and perhaps as many more hold residential real estate. Approximately 270,000 proprietors own the unincorporated factories, but how many have invested in corporate securities is enigmatical. Tax lists show that the number of families having large amounts of wealth is small, but fail to give the clue to the diffusion of capital. Although it may be crudely stated that there are over eighteen thousand rich families in the country, this knowledge is of little value without some definition of " rich ". There are probably more than four thousand millionaires. To attempt, therefore, to estimate the distribution of incomes from property would be absurd.

If it is impossible to determine the number of persons who own productive property, it is not quite so difficult to approximate the earning power of capital. " Seven trust companies in New York, with a total capitalization of $25,-375,000, made during the period between November 10, 1910, and December 21, 1911, $10,436,300, or 45.1 per

---

[1] Watkins, *American Economic Association*, 1907, vol. 8, pp. 143, 145.

cent. These figures are taken from the reports on those
dates and include the dividends paid by these companies in
that interval." [1]   Thus the annual rate of return on the
par value of stock was close to forty per cent. It must be
remembered, however, when considering banking institutions of any class that the " surplus " really is capital.
Even with this reservation, the fact that the thirty-six New
York City Trust Companies in 1909 earned a net income
of 36.88 per cent of their capitalization, and paid dividends averaging 22.49 per cent shows well what great return may be reaped by investors in a comparatively " sure
thing ". [2]

Other enterprises are not so highly remunerative. During the year ending June 30, 1910, for example, no dividend was paid on over thirty-three per cent of the stock
of the railways, and less than four per cent on thirty-nine
per cent. The successful companies seem to distribute
from six to eight per cent. [3]   In Table XXXIX is shown the
capital stock, funded debt, dividends and interest, or net
corporate income, for various forms of enterprise. The
return to stockholders varies from 1.62 per cent of the par
value of capitalization in the case of independent telephone
companies to 14.52 per cent for private banks and a rate
higher still for express companies; but in almost every industry there are some concerns which earn even less than
the interest on the bonds. The most important item in the
table is the last, the returns of the 270,202 corporations
reporting to the Commissioner of Internal Revenue. The
average rate of interest on bonds paid by commercial con-

---

[1] *Wall Street Journal,* 16 Jan., 1912.

[2] Compiled from reports in the *Financial Age,* 3 Jan., 1910, pp. 34, 35,
vol. xxi.

[3] *Statistics of Railways* for year ending June 30, 1910, p. 56.

TABLE XXXIX

EARNINGS OF INVESTED CAPITAL　(*References on opposite page.*)

I. Class of investment.	II. Date of returns.	III. Capital stock.	IV. Bonded debt.	V. Total capital or capitalization.	VI. Dividends.	VII. Rate of dividends.	VIII. Interest on bonded debt.	IX. Rate of interest on bonds.	X. Net income.
1. Interest bearing debt of the United States ..	30 June, 1911	......	915,353,190	......	......	......	21,336,673	2.33	......
2. Debts of states and minor civil divisions	1902	......	1,864,978,483	......	......	......	89,664,985	4.81	......
	year ending								
3. National banks (6,984)	30 June, 1910	963,457,549	......	963,457,549	105,898,622	10.99	......	......	154,167,489
4. State banks (6,708)	"	303,415,173	......	303,415,173	32,205,248	10.61	......	......	......
5. Private banks (359)	"	6,987,650	......	6,987,650	1,014,937	14.52	......	......	......
6. Loan and trust companies (807)	"	296,762,603	......	296,762,603	37,434,654	12.61	......	......	......
	year ending								
7. Stocks savings banks	30 June, 1910	68,320,822	......	68,320,822	5,367,707	7.86	......	......	......
Deposits and "interest"	"	......	......	799,922,404	16,217,317	3.56	......	......	......
8. Mutual savings banks, deposits and "interest"	"	......	......	3,360,563,843	111,360,310	3.92	......	......	......
9 Insurance companies (214)	1910	43,446,277	......	43,446,277	2,023,028	4.66	......	......	......
Dividends to policy holders	1910	......	......	3,832,430,782	75,353,638	1.97	......	......	......
10. Steam railways	1910	8,113,657,380	10,303,474,858	18,417,132,238	405,771,416	5.00	399,582,056	3.88	......
11. Street railways	1907	2,097,708,856	1,677,063,240	3,774,772,096	54,485,274	2.60	71,468,788	4.26	......
	year ending								
12. Pullman Company	30 June, 1911	120,000,000	......	120,000,000	9,446,230	7.87	......	......	11,416,677
13. Express companies	1910	69,523,300	36,000,000	105,523,300	32,703,831	[47.04]	860,580	2.39	15,367,572
14. All Bell system of telephone companies	1910	344,645,400	224,791,700	569,437,100	25,160,800	7.30	11,556,900	5.14	39,437,500
15. Independent Telephone Cos.	1907	218,106,619	104,888,339	322,995,558	3,531,733	1.62	4,788,700	4.56	......
16. Western Union Telegraph Co.	1911	99,817,100	40,572,000	140,389,100	2,989,696	3.00	1,687,830	4.16	7,274,900
17. Central electric light and power stations	1907	741,317,497	626,021,339	1,367,338,836	19,300,572	2.60	27,991,762	4.47	......
18. Mines and quarries, incorporated companies.	1902	2,902,835,544	314,883,914	3,217,719,458	72,416,013	2.49	13,603,924	4.32	......
19. 185 industrial combinations	1900	2,876,683,109	216,412,759	3,093,095,868	135,126,612	4.70	......	......	......
20. 270,202 corporations paying special excise tax	1910	57,886,430,519	30,715,336,008	88,601,766,527	......	......	......	......	3,360,250,643

cerns, as shown by the figures in the table, is 3.99 per cent; at this rate the bonds of these corporations would pay in the course of the year $1,225,541,900. Adding this sum to the official net income gives $4,585,893,000, or a return of 5.176 per cent on the total capitalization of $88,601,-766,527.[1] These figures are particularly significant in that the receipts of companies due to intercorporate holdings of stock are deducted in finding the net revenue; thus the in-

[1] It may be interesting to note that the census estimate of the total wealth of the United States in 1900 was $88,517,306,775. *Statistical Abstract of the United States* for 1910, p. 589. Compare this with the nominal capital of the corporations in 1910, $88,601,766,527.

REFERENCES FOR TABLE XXXIX:

1. *American Year-Book*, p. 27.
2. *Wealth, Debt, and Taxation*, Twelfth Census, pp. 142, 221.
3. *Report of the Comptroller of the Currency*, 1910, p. 334.
4, 5, 6. *Ibid.*, p. 831. (Includes only those paying dividends on stock.)
7. *Ibid.*, pp. 743, 783, 831.
8. *Ibid.*, pp. 739, 783.
9. F. L. Hoffman, *Quarterly Publications of the American Statistical Association*, no. 95, vol. xii, pp. 732, 735, 751. (Includes forty-three mutual companies. "Admitted assets" entered in table as capital stock. Only 66 of the companies paid dividends, their rate being 8.48 per cent on the $23,842,441 stock.)
10. *Statistics of Railways*, 1910, pp. 50, 51, 55, 57.
11. *Street Railways, Special Census Report*, 1907, pp. 102, 103.
12. *Preliminary Abstract of Statistics of Common Carriers*, 1911, p. 55.
13. *Special Report, Interstate Commerce Commission, Express Companies*, 1910, pp. 15, 30. (Includes $24,000,000 extra dividend by Wells, Fargo Co.)
14. *American Year-Book*, 1911, p. 549.
15. *Special Census Report, Telephone Companies*, 1907, pp. 57, 59. (Excludes inter-company payments.)
16. *American Year-Book*, 1911, p. 548.
17. *Special Census Report, Central Electric Light and Power Stations*, p. 61.
18. *Census Report, Mines and Quarries*, 1902, p. 88.
19. *Census of Manufactures*, 1900, pt. i, p. lxxix.
20. *Report of the Commissioner of Internal Revenue*, 1911, p. 75.

come as reported by the Commissioner of Internal Revenue
has eliminated duplications.

Even with this excellent information as to the earnings
of all the corporations doing business in the United States,
it is impossible to find the net earnings of capital, because
the necessary data are lacking for such important industries
as farming, the renting of real estate, store-keeping, and a
host of minor enterprises. For example, in the field of
agriculture, there is no way of determining how much of
the $8,900,000,000 worth of produce in 1909 was due to
the labor of the farmer, and how much to his land and implements; and, indeed, the value of some of the farm products reappears in the dividends of such corporations as the
great milk companies. Moreover, the capitalization of corporations is no criterion of the actual investment.

A triple conclusion is, therefore, confirmed at every turn.
First, that the number of individuals enjoying incomes
from capital is unknown, though large; second, that the
total national income from capital cannot be accurately determined; third, that as a consequence, it is futile to attempt to describe, in any way definite enough to be valuable,
the distribution of incomes from property in the United
States.[1]

---

[1] The same may be said of incomes from the right of private property. From the Surrogates' books in New York, and the Probate
records in Connecticut, it would be possible to compile a table showing
the distribution of inheritances by size, but to-day the state of New
York keeps no record of either the number or the aggregate value of
estates assessed, much less anything more detailed.

CHAPTER VIII

SUMMARY AND CONCLUSION

FOR the intelligent discussion of many social questions which are pressing more and more their claim upon public attention, a clear concept of the distribution of incomes among the individuals and families of the United States is necessary. The more elaborate and exact this concept is, the more useful it may become; but, for many purposes, all that is requisite is a simple presentation of the number of adult males or of families in each income group, the groups being definite and preferably limited in range to one hundred dollars, at least as far as the thousand-dollar mark. It would be well, if possible, to draw a distinction between rewards of labor, and returns from the ownership of property; inheritance and gifts, being essentially transfers of revenue from capital, are not particularly important in this connection. Although a great mass of wage statistics is at hand, most of this material is of little value in determining annual earnings; but there have been some important compilations of the classified weekly pay of factory operatives in the United States as a whole, and in the commonwealths of Massachusetts, New Jersey, Kansas, and Wisconsin, as well as the unique reports from labor organizations in New York, and several excellent special studies, notably the *Eighteenth Annual Report of the Bureau of Labor,* and the returns to the Kansas and Iowa questionnaires. These publications, however, treat only the compensation of labor; and there is scant basis for an investigation of the division of the earnings of capital. The incomplete success, which has attended the serious attempts to treat statistically the distribution either of incomes or of earnings in the United States, is due to this surprising lack of data.

It has not been the aim of this essay to solve the problem, but rather to depict the deplorable dearth of information on a subject so vital to the welfare of the country. Some conclusions have been reached, but they must be considered tentative, and accepted, if at all, only with their qualifications. It is important to note that somewhere between four and five-tenths of the industrial families of the United States are dependent for support entirely upon the father-husband; probably the same proportion does not hold for agricultural districts. In the second place, the purchasing power of pay in manufactures in New York has nearly doubled since the close of the Civil War; presumably this is also true of other industries, and of other states. On the other hand, in the last twenty years, the gain of REAL wages, among factory operatives, and among trade-unionists in New York, seems to have been slight. A consideration of the evidence found in all the available reports, leads to the conclusion that in 1904, and probably at the present time, at least half of the males aged sixteen or more, engaged in gainful occupations were earning less than $626 a year. This statement cannot be considered a description of the distribution of incomes, for there is sometimes a wide difference between the earnings of the head of a household and its actual receipts. It neither refutes nor confirms the belief of Dr. Spahr, that in 1892, 11,000,000, or seven-eighths of the American families, had incomes under $1,200, but it is interesting to note that of the nineteen and a half-million men tabulated in Table XXXVII, hardly one-twelfth were annually earning more than $1,000 (or $1,043). Another striking fact is that the grand list of New Britain showed about one-eighth of the families having property worth at least $5,000, exactly the proportion found by Dr. Spahr for New York State eighteen years before, and by him used as the foundation of his estimate.[1]

This estimate of at least one-half the adult males earning less than $626 per annum is in perfect harmony with the results of Professor Nearing,[2] provided his rather questionable deduction for unemployment be ignored. The important point to note here, however, is that in this essay account was taken roughly of agricultural laborers and of farm families, which gives the conclusion a far greater scope than that confined to industrial workers north of the Mason-Dixon line and east of the Rockies.

The remarkable similarity between the results of Spahr for the United States and of Leroy-Beaulieu for Paris has been noted; for this country 87.5 per cent of the families were said to have incomes under $1,200, for Paris 89.02 under 7,000 francs ($1,351). The earnings of men are of course not comparable with the family incomes of Parisians. Taking only the industrial workers in Table XXXVII, it is noticable that about sixty-three per cent were earning less than $626 per year and over ninety per cent less than $1,044. In Paris the incomes of nearly forty-nine per cent of the families were under 2,100 francs ($505.30), and of 74.60 per cent under 3,500 francs ($675.-50). Although there seems to be no way of accurately comparing the two scales, as the earnings of industrial workingmen are being contrasted with the incomes of ALL the families of the French capital, the situation in America appears to be no worse.

[1] *Vide supra*, opening pages of chapter v.

[2] *Vide supra*, p. 75.

It appeared that, in 1905, over one-half, probably six-tenths of the Prussians belonged to families having incomes under 2,700 M. ($643). As 56.48 per cent of the inhabitants of this principality lived in households no member of which annually received 900 M. ($214), it is safe to conclude that money wages are far higher in the United States than in Germany. Similarly, so far as money alone is concerned, the Americans are certainly better off than the English, for it will be remembered that the "inhabited house tax" showed that about four-fifths of the English families were in tenements the rental value of which would indicate an income under £140 ($681).

In all these comparisons no attention has been paid to price levels in the different localities or at the different periods of time. Without fuller knowledge, it is folly to compare the welfare of American workers with that of people of other countries, for the statistics are absolutely incomparable; earnings of men and family incomes are essentially distinct, mental traits vary from place to place, purchasing power of money constantly changes, and, finally, the conclusions as to wages are all uncertain. This much, however, can be said, the money earnings of American men, seem to be at least equal to the money incomes of families in France, England, and Prussia.

Vague as must be these conclusions as to the earnings of labor, even less is known of incomes from property. More than ten million individuals are doubtless recipients of small dividends from savings banks and life insurance companies, probably over eight million enjoy returns from agricultural and residential real estate, but how many are interested in incorporated companies none can tell. Eighteen thousand men are rich enough to have their names entered in the *Financial Red Book,* and over four thousand were millionaires in 1892. But these bits of information are no sound basis for studying the distribution of incomes from property.

The conclusion of the whole matter is this. Knowledge of the distribution of incomes is vital to sane legislative direction of progress. In a form definite enough for practical use, this knowledge does not exist. No time should be wasted in obtaining this knowledge.

CHAPTER IX

A Suggestion

FROM the foregoing discussion two facts should be clear: first, that up to the present time there has been no satisfactory study of the distribution of incomes in the United States; and, second, that the material for such a study is not now available. It remains to suggest a simple and effective method of obtaining this material.

A well-administered, progressive income tax might easily furnish the clue. But it must be remembered that taxes are not imposed for the purpose of gathering sociological data.[1] Neither the English nor the Prussian imposts allow of precise translation into terms of distribution of incomes, and the Comptroller of the State of New York cannot even say how many estates are assessed in a given year. Suppose that the Constitutional amendment now apparently approaching ratification be adopted, and a tax imposed under it, if the policy of tapping at the source be adopted, the records will completely fail to reveal the distribution of incomes. Taxation, therefore, promises slight aid.

Obviously the simplest expedient is to ask at the census what the income of the family, or of its head and of each contributing member, is. But this plan is probably imprac-

---

[1] The income-tax law of Wisconsin, the first assessment under which is not complete at this writing, exempts $800 to individuals. Thus a summary of the assessments will not show the distribution of incomes; other deductions will make even more difficult the estimate of distribution.

ticable at the present time. It is so " inquisitorial " that it is " un-American ". Such a question would certainly encounter resentment, and, perhaps, misrepresentation if not defiance. Moreover, it is probable that many of the very rich do not know exactly what their income is; the poor are very frequently unable to say what they have earned in the course of the year. So it seems that, at least for the present, the direct question is not feasible.

There is nothing original in the plan about to be proposed except the technique of its application. But in the technique lies the secret of accuracy of approximation to the facts.

First, the families of the United States may be divided into two large classes, farm families, and non-agricultural families. Sixty-four per cent of the agricultural households own their homes, nearly sixty-four per cent of the non-farm families rent their dwellings.[1] As to the farm families, the recent *Census of Agriculture* called for the following information concerning the individual farms in 1909:

1. Total value of products at the farm.

2. Amount spent in cash for farm labor (exclusive of housework).

3. Amount spent for feed for domestic animals.

4. Amount spent for fertilizers.

5. Estimated value of house rent and board furnished farm laborers in addition to cash wages.

6. Whether the operator owned and rented other farm land.

7. Total value of products not fed to live stock.

It will readily be seen that if, from the value of products not fed to live stock, were subtracted the amount spent in

---

[1] *Abstract of the Twelfth Census*, p. 28.

cash for labor, the cost of purchased feed and fertilizers, and the value of the accommodations furnished to the help, there would be left a fairly close approximation to the income of the farm family. If the next Census include one additional question, calling for the rent paid by those who hire their places, or for the interest on mortgages, the information for determining the net return to the household from working the farm will be complete.[1] The revenues thus determined should be classified according to size, and, also, with regard to whether the operator holds other land from which he derives income, owns simply the farm he tills, or hires the property. Since the additional question concerning rent or interest on mortgage is no more "inquisitorial" than those already asked and answered concerning the value of products, the value of the farm, and the amount of mortgage indebtedness, it should prove itself practical. A classification of the net returns calculated on this basis would not, to be sure, give an exact summary of the distribution of incomes among the agricultural families, for some farmers have other investments than land, but it would approach much more closely to the facts than any knowledge available at present, and would be a valuable first step.

The problem of the distribution of incomes among the non-agricultural families can probably be best approached through the rental values of their living accommodations. To ask the rent paid for a hired dwelling, or the rental value of an owned home, is hardly more bold than to inquire whether the house is mortgaged. An intelligent agent could form an accurate opinion of the correctness of the

---

[1] For real accuracy a further deduction should be made for seeds, insurance, depreciation of implements, and part of taxes. The plan aims at the simplest way of securing approximately correct results, without cumbering the schedules.

reply. An ignorant laborer could answer this question much more easily than one calling for a knowledge of his year's earnings. This inquiry could, therefore, easily be carried on the Population Schedule without incurring much risk of misrepresentation or of opposition. The interpretation of the returns in terms of the distribution of incomes, although not so simple as may at first appear, is entirely feasible.

It is well known that as the incomes of families increase the average expenditure for rent rises in absolute amount but decreases relatively. For example, in 1890, there were collected in St. Louis budgets which showed the total earnings and the rents paid by 254 households. As these were industrial people, the error is probably not great in treating the total earnings as the family income. On this basis the following table has been compiled:

TABLE XL[1]

RELATION OF RENT TO FAMILY EARNINGS, ST. LOUIS, 1890

I.	II.	III.
Family earnings.	Average rent,	Per cent. of earnings spent for rent.
$ 300 but under $400...................	$84	24
400 " " 500.....	87	19
500 " " 600...................	104	19
600 " " 700...................	108	17
700 " " 800...................	117	16
800 " " 900...................	124	15
900 " " 1,000................	125	13
1,000 " " 1,100................	143	14
1,100 " " 12,00................	154	13
1,200 and over	165	10

[1] Compiled from the individual returns in the *Annual Report of the Missouri Bureau of Labor Statistics*, 1890, pp. 400 *et seq.*

In addition to the facts in Table XL the distribution of rents among these families is known to be that in Table XLI.

TABLE XLI

DISTRIBUTION OF RENTS AMONG 254 ST. LOUIS FAMILIES, 1890

I.	II.
Rent.	Number of families.
$50 but under $70.....................................	4
70 " " 90...................................	34
90 " " 110...................................	74
110 " " 130...................................	70
130 " " 150...................................	37
150 " " 170...................................	16
170 " " 190...................................	9
160 and over	10

Is it permissible to reason thus? If the income is $500 and under $600 the proportion spent for rent is 19 per cent, if the earnings are $600 but under $700, 17 per cent. Thus the proper rent to be paid from a $600 income is about 18 per cent of $600 or $108. From the table it appears that 38 rents are less than $90; 74 are between $90 and $110; eighteen-twentieths of 74 is 66; therefore about 104 rents are under $108, or the earnings of 104 families are less than $600. The answer is to be found in the following table which compares the number in each earnings group as thus computed, and as actually enumerated.

TABLE XLII

DISTRIBUTION OF INCOMES AMONG 254 ST. LOUIS FAMILIES AS COMPUTED FROM
RENTALS BY FIRST METHOD, AND AS ENUMERATED

I.	II.	III.	IV.
	Number in group.		Difference II–III.
Income group.	Computed from rents.	Enumerated.	
Under $600..........	104	65	+39
$600 under 800	57	86	—29
800 " 1,000	30	54	—24
1,000 " 1,200 ...	33	22	+11
1,200 and over.	30	27	+ 3
Totals	254	254	+53 —53

The experiment makes it clear that this method of estimating the distribution of incomes from the classified returns of rents is not at all satisfactory. The trouble probably lies in the tendency for rents to concentrate on multiples of six and twelve.

Is there not a law of the relation of rent to income?
Certainly. If, in the case of these particular St. Louis families the total earnings be measured on the X axis, and the
rent paid on the Y axis, and if the origin is at (0,0), then
the law of the relation of rent to income is $y = 0.055x +
74.30$.[1] In other words, to find the normal rent for a given
income, multiply the earnings by 0.055 and add $74.30.
Applying this law, and using the actual rents of the individual families, instead of interpolating as above, the following approximation of the distribution of incomes is
obtained:

[1] Calculated by the method of moments.

TABLE XLIII

DISTRIBUTION OF INCOMES AMONG 254 ST. LOUIS FAMILIES, AS COMPUTED BY
MEANS OF THE EQUATION OF REGRESSION

I.	II.	III.	IV.	V.
		Number in group.		
Income group.	Corresponding rents.	Computed from rents.	Enumeration.	Difference III-IV.
Under $600..........	Under $107.30 ...	76	65	+11
$600 and under $800 ..	$107.31– 118.30..	46	86	–40
800 " " 1,000 ..	118.31– 129.30..	60	54	+ 6
1,000 " " 1,200 ..	129.31– 140.30..	20	22	– 2
1,200 and over........	140.31 and over .	52	27	+25
Totals	....	254	254	+42
				–42

This estimate is not much preferable to the other. By the first method fifty-three cases were misplaced, by the second, forty-two.

Probably the best approximation can be obtained by the method exemplified in Table XLIV. After shuffling thoroughly the cards on which were entered the rents and family earnings of these 254 St. Louis families, a random sample was taken without particular reference to size. It included 124 cards. Sorting showed the distribution of rents and incomes to be that recorded in Table XLIV, A. Section B of the table was next computed to show the percent distribution of earnings among the families in each rent group. The first line in section C gives the distribution of the families in the rent groups as determined by the enumeration. Using the percents in section B, these numbers in the first line of section C were apportioned among the various income groups for

TABLE XLIV

COMPUTATION OF DISTRIBUTION OF INCOMES FROM DISTRIBUTION OF RENTS, 254 ST. LOUIS FAMILIES

A. Numerical Distribution of Rents and Incomes in Sample

I. Income.	II. $50, under $70.	III. $70, under $90.	IV. $90, under $110.	V. $110, under $130.	VI. $130, under $150.	VII. $150, under $170.	VIII. $170, under $190.	IX. $190 and over.	X. Totals.	XI.	XII.
				Rents.							
Under $600	1	11	7	7	2	......	1	....	29	...	......
$600, under $800	....	3	18	11	4	1	......	1	37	...	......
800, under 1,000	....	1	4	12	5	2	2	....	26	...	......
1,000, under 1,200	....	1	....	1	3	2	4	1	12	...	......
1,200 and over	....	....	2	5	4	3	2	4	20	...	......
Totals	1	16	31	36	18	8	9	5	124	....	......

B. Per cent Distribution of Incomes in each Rent Group

Income	$50, under $70.	$70, under $90.	$90, under $110.	$110, under $130.	$130, under $150.	$150, under $170.	$170, under $190.	$190 and over.	Totals.		
Under $600	100	69	23	19	11	.....	11	....	....	....	......
$600, under $800	....	19	58	31	22	13	......				
800, under 1,000	....	6	13	33	28	25	22				
1,000, under 1,200	....	6	..	3	17	25	45	20			
1,200 and over	....		6	14	22	37	22	80			
Totals	100	100	100	100	100	100	100	100	....	....	......

C. Numerical Distribution of Incomes among 254 St. Louis Families Computed from Actual Distribution of all Rents and from B, Compared with Results of Actual Enumeration

									Estimate.	Enumeration.	Difference X–XI.
Distribution of rents (entire enumeration)	4	34	74	70	37	16	9	10	254		
Income—											
Under $600	4	23	17	13	4	......	1	....	62	65	− 3
$600, under $800	....	7	43	22	8	2	......	....	82	86	− 4
800, under 1,000	....	2	10	23	11	4	2	....	52	54	− 2
1,000, under 1,200	....	2	....	2	6	4	4	2	20	22	− 2
1,200 and over	....	....	4	10	8	6	2	8	38	27	+ 11
Totals	4	34	74	70	37	16	9	10	254	254	{ + 11 / − 11 }

TABLE XLV

COMPUTATION OF DISTRIBUTION OF INCOMES FROM THE DISTRIBUTION OF RENTS, 391 NEW YORK FAMILIES

A. Numerical Distribution of Rents and Incomes in Sample

I.	II.	III.	IV.	V.	VI.	VII.	VIII.	IX.	X.	XI.	XII.	XIII.
	Rents.											
Incomes.	Under $110.	$110 but under $130.	$130 but under $150.	$150 but under $170.	$170 but under $190.	$190 but under $210.	$210 but under $230.	$230 but under $250.	$250 and over.	Totals.		
Under $600............	1	4	3	2	1	1	....	....	....	12	....	....
$600 but under $800......	....	10	15	13	6	9	2	....	2	57	....	....
800 but under 1,000......	4	8	7	14	7	8	7	....	3	58	....	....
1,000 but under 1,200......	1	....	3	4	5	4	1	3	....	21	....	....
1,200 and over	..	....	1	1	....	1	2	1	6	12	....	....
Totals.................	6	22	29	34	19	23	12	4	11	160	....	.. ..

B. Per cent Distribution of Incomes in Each Rent Group

Incomes	Under $110	$110–130	$130–150	$150–170	$170–190	$190–210	$210–230	$230–250	$250 and over			
Under $600........	17	18	10	6	5	4	....	....	....	..	....	....
$600 but under $800......	....	45	53	38	32	39	17	....	18	....	....	....
800 but under 1,000......	66	37	24	41	37	35	58	....	27	....	....	....
1,000 but under 1,200.....	17	....	10	12	26	18	8	75	....	....	....	....
1,200 and over	....	..	3	3	....	4	17	25	55	....	....	....
Totals....	100	100	100	100	100	100	100	100	100	....	....	....

C. Numerical Distribution of Incomes among 391 New York City Families Computed from Actual Distribution of Rents and from B, and Compared with Results of Enumeration

											Estimate.	Enumeration (see Table).	Differences XI–XII.
Distribution of rents (entire enumeration)	17	51	70	100	41	49	24	13	26		391		
Incomes—													
Under $600	3	9	7	6	2	2	....	....	....		29	26	3
$600 but under $800....	....	23	37	38	13	19	4	....	5		139	151	—12
800 but under 1,000....	11	19	17	41	15	17	14	..	7		141	134	7
1,000 but under 1,200....	3	....	7	12	11	9	2	9	....		53	50	3
1,200 and over	....	....	2	3	....	2	4	4	14		29	30	— 1
Totals.................	17	51	70	100	41	49	24	13	26		391	391	$\{^{+13}_{-13}$

each rent group.[1] Then the totals for the income groups
were determined and placed in column X.   It will be noticed
that these agree much more closely with the figures actually found by the enumeration than the results of either of
the two previous estimates, the net number of misplacements being 11, as contrasted with 53 and 42.   An even
better result was obtained for the 391 New York families
with a random sample of 160, there being 13 misplacements
net.   If there were available for the test data involving a
greater number of cases, the accuracy would doubtless be
far greater.

A simple plan, then, of obtaining an approximate estimate of the distribution of incomes among the families of
the United States is briefly this:

1. The distribution of incomes among farm families may
be obtained from the data of the *Census of Agriculture,* if
a new question calling for rent paid or interest on mortgage, be added to the schedule; and if, in compilation, the
incomes of the farm families—computed by subtracting
from the total value of products not fed to live stock, the
wages and value of accommodation extended to farm laborers, the cost of feed and fertilizer purchased, and the rent
or interest on the mortgage[2]—be classified according to

---

[1] For example, take column III.   According to the first line of section C, the actual count showed thirty-four families paying rents of
$70 but less than $90.   Section B reveals the fact that sixty-nine per
cent of these thirty-four families have incomes under $600.   There-
fore, in column III, in the line for families having incomes below $600,
is placed the number twenty-three (sixty-nine per cent of thirty-four).
Similarly, nineteen per cent (seven) had incomes of $600 but under
$800, six per cent (two) had incomes of $800 but under $1,000, six per
cent (two) had incomes of $1,000 but under $1,200, and none had an
income of $1,200 or over.   In the same way the other columns of sec-
tion C were filled out.

[2] Cost of insurance, seed, taxes, and depreciation of implements
should be deducted if they can be obtained in the census.

size and to the condition of the operator—whether he owns or hires his farm, and whether he possesses other farm property from which he secures a return.

2. The distribution of incomes among the non-agricultural households is to be determined by adding to the population schedule a question calling for the rent or the rental value of the house or tenement occupied by the family. A supplementary study must be made of a large number of households to ascertain exactly the distribution of incomes among the families in each rent group. Such a study could be made a year or two before the Census by the Bureau of Labor; enough families could be found willing to co-operate to give a sufficient basis for generalization. The results of this study should be tabulated separately for the small and large municipalities of each commonwealth. Similarly the Census returns should be separated for different-sized communities in each state, and for families in which the father-husband is and is not the only wage-earner.

The combination of the results of these two investigations would not be an exact summary of the distribution of incomes in the United States. The results would not likely be such as to aid in the development of wage theory; but the approximation would probably be so close to the facts that it would be a material aid in the solution of several great social questions.

BIBLIOGRAPHY

LIST OF PUBLICATIONS TO WHICH REFERENCE IS MADE
IN THIS ESSAY

I. Publications of the United States Government, Washington, D. C.
  A. Census Publications.
    1. Tenth Census of the United States.
      Public Indebtedness, Vol. VII.
    2. Twelfth Census of the United States.
      Abstract of the Twelfth Census, 1904.
      Agriculture, Vols. V and VI, 1902.
      Manufactures, four volumes, 1900.
        Special Reports—
      Mines and Quarries, 1902.
      Telephones and Telegraphs, 1902.
      Employees and Wages, 1903.
      Occupations, 1904.
      Wealth, Debt, and Taxation, 1904.
      Manufactures, 1905, four volumes.
      Religious Bodies, 1906.
      Central Electric Light and Power Stations, 1907.
      Express Business in the United States, 1907.
      *Statistics of Employees, Executive Civil Service of the
        United States,* 1907. Bulletin No. 94.
      Street and Electric Railways, 1907.
      Telephone Industry, 1907.
      The Shipping Industry.
      Mortality Statistics, annual.
    3. Thirteenth Census of the United States.
      Advance Statement, General Data on Agriculture.
      Bulletin, Manufactures; United States.
  B. Publications prepared by the Department of Commerce and
    Labor.
    Bulletin of the Bureau of Labor. Bi-monthly.
    Eighteenth Annual Report of the Commissioner of Labor.
    1903.

Investigation of Telephone Companies. Sen. Doc., 380, 61st Cong., 2nd Ses., 1910.

Report on Strike at the Bethlehem Steel Works. Sen. Doc., 521, 61st Cong., 2nd Ses., 1910.

Report on Condition of Woman and Child Wage-Earners in the United States. Sen. Doc., 645, 61st Cong., 2nd Ses., 1911, 1912.

Statistical Abstract of the United States, annual.

C. Publications prepared by the Interstate Commerce Commission. Sen. Doc., 188, 58th Cong., 3rd Ses. *Ownership of R. R. Stock,* 1905.

Statistics of the Railways, annual.

Preliminary Abstract of Statistics of Common Carriers for Year ending June 30, 1911 (1912).

Statistics of Express Companies for Year Ending June 30, 1910 (1911).

D. Publications prepared by the Treasury Department.
Report of the Comptroller of Currency.
Report of the Commissioner of Internal Revenue, annual.

E. Report of the Select Committee on Wages and Prices of Commodities. Sen. Doc., 847, 61st Cong., 3rd Ses., 1911.

F. Year Book, Department of Agriculture, annual.

G. Report, Commissioner of Education, annual.

II. Publications of State Authorities.

Connecticut, *Report of Bank Commissioner,* annual.

Illinois, *Report of Bureau of Labor Statistics,* biennial.

Iowa, *Report of Bureau of Labor Statistics,* biennial.

Kansas, *Report of Bureau of Labor and Industry,* annual.

Massachusetts, *Statistics of Manufactures,* annual.

Michigan, *Report of the Bureau of Labor,* annual.

Missouri, *Report of the Bureau of Labor Statistics,* annual.

New Jersey, *Report, Bureau of Statistics of Labor and Industries,* annual.

New York, *Report of Bureau of Labor Statistics,* annual.
Report of Commissioner of Labor, annual.
Bulletin, Department of Labor, quarterly.
Report of the Comptroller, annual.
Census, 1865.

Ohio, *Report of the Bureau of Labor Statistics,* annual.

Pennsylvania, *Report of the Secretary of Internal Affairs,* Pt. III, *Industrial Statistics,* annual.

Tennessee, *Report of the Bureau of Labor Statistics and Mines,* annual.

Washington, *Report of the Bureau of Labor Statistics and Factory Inspection,* biennial.

Wisconsin, *Report of the Bureau of Labor and Industrial Statistics, Pt. VIII, Manufacturing Returns,* biennial.

III. Other Official Publications.

Annual Minutes of Various Methodist Episcopal Conferences.

Report of the Commissioners of His Majesty's Inland Revenue, annual.

IV. Private Publications.

Adams, H. C., *Science of Finance.* New York, 1898, 1906.

Adams, T. S., and Sumner, H. L., *Labor Problems.* New York, 1905.

Beaulieu, Paul Leroy-, *Essai sur la repartition des richesses,* fourth ed. Paris, 1896.

Chapin, Robert C., *The Standard of Living in New York City.* Charities Publication Committee, New York, 1909.

Clark, J. B., *Essentials of Economic Theory.* New York, 1907.

Johnson, J. F., *Money and Currency.* Boston, 1905.

Nearing, Scott, *Wages in the United States.* New York, 1911.

Ryan, J. A., *A Living Wage.* New York, 1906.

Seager, H. R., *Introduction to Economics.* New York, 1904, 1907.

Seligman, E. R. A., *Principles of Economics.* New York, 1905.

Spahr, Chas. B., *Present Distribution of Wealth in the United States.* New York, 1896.

Streightoff, F. H., *Standard of Living among the Industrial People of America.* Boston, 1911.

Watkins, G. P., *The Growth of Large Fortunes.* Publications of the American Economic Association, 3rd Series, vol. vii, no. 4. New York, 1907.

Wright, C. D., ed., *Report of Committee on Salaries, Tenure and Pensions of Public School Teachers in the United States.* National Education Association.

Financial Red Book of America. New York, 1905.

V. Periodicals.

American Medical Compend.

American Year Book for 1911.

The Financial Age.

Jahrbücher für National Oekonomie und Statistik.

Journal of the Royal Statistical Society.

Political Science Quarterly.

Quarterly Publications, American Statistical Association.

Wall Street Journal.

ADDITIONAL REFERENCES

I. BOOKS

Brooks, J. G., *The Social Unrest: Studies in Labor and Social Movements*. New York, 1903.

Carver, T. N., *Distribution of Wealth*. New York.

Cherbuliez, J., *Riche ou pauvre, exposition succincte des causes et des effets de la distribution actuelle des richesses sociales*. Paris, 1840.

Clark, J. B., *The Distribution of Wealth: a Theory of Wages, Interest, and Profit*. New York, 1899.

Collins, J. A., *Distribution of Wealth in the United States*. Sen. Doc., 75, 55th Cong., 2nd Ses., 1898.

Commons, J. R., *The Distribution of Wealth*. New York, 1893.

Conrad, J., *Handwörterbuch der Staatswissenschaften*.

Giffen, R., *Progress of the Working Classes*. London, 1885.

Matthews, B. C., *Our Irrational Distribution of Wealth*. New York, 1908.

Money, L. G. Chiozza-, M. P., *Riches and Poverty*. London, 1905.

Moore, H. L., *Laws of Wages*. New York, 1911.

Mulhall, M. G., *Industries and Wealth of Nations*. New York, 1896.

Pareto, W., *Cours d'economie politique*. Lausanne and Paris, 1897.

Smart, W., *Distribution of Income*. London, 1899.

Smith, R. Mayo-, *The Science of Statistics*, 2 vols. New York.

Sergeew, C., *Die Verteilung der Güter in einigen Kantonen der Schweiz*. Basel, 1889.

Underwood, J. H., *The Distribution of Ownership*. Columbia University Studies in History, Economics and Public Law, New York, 1907.

Webb, A. D., *New Dictionary of Statistics*. New York, 1911.

Cost of Living in American Towns. Report into Working Class Rent, Housing, Wages, etc. Cd. 5609. London, 1911.

II. ARTICLES

Bowley, A. L., "Suggestions for the International Comparison of Wages by the Use of the Median." *Journal Royal Statistical Society,* vol. 72, p. 718. 1909.

Cannan, E., "Division of Income." *Quarterly Journal of Economics,* vol. 19, p. 341. 1905.

Carver, T. N., "How Ought Wealth to he Distributed?" *Atlantic Monthly,* vol. 97, p. 727.

Edwards, E. J., "The New Salaried Class." *American Monthly Review of Reviews,* vol. 32, p. 339. 1905.

Forbes, E. A., "Is the Doctor a Shylock?" *World's Work,* vol. 14, p. 8892. 1907.

Giffen, R., " The Wealth of the Empire and How it Should be Used."
    J. R. S. S., vol. 66. 1903.
Goschen, G. J., " Increase of Moderate Incomes." *J. R. S. S.,* vol. 50.
    1887.
Harris, W. J., and Lake, K. A., " Estimates of the Realizable Wealth
    of the United Kingdom." *J. R. S. S.,* vol. 69, p. 709. 1906.
Holmes, G. K., " How Far Should Family Wealth be Encouraged and
    Conserved?" *American Journal of Sociology,* vol. 14, p. 823.
    1909.
Hutchinson, J. G., " Can the Working Class Save?" *Nineteenth Cen-
    tury,* vol. 63, p. 285.
Lorenz, M. O., " Methods of Measuring the Concentration of Wealth."
    American Statistical Association, vol. 9, p. 209. 1905.
Moore, H. L., " The Differential Law of Wages." *J. R. S. S.,* vol. 70.
    p. 638. 1907.
Moore, H. L., " Variability of Wages." *Political Science Quarterly,*
    vol. 22, p. 61. 1907.
Persons, W. M., " Present Distribution of Wealth." *Q. J. Ec.,* vol. 23,
    p. 416. 1909.
Powers, L. G., " The Assets of the United States." *Am. J. Soc.,* vol.
    14, p. 171. 1908.
Watkins, G. P., " An Interpretation of Certain Statistical Evidence of
    Concentration of Wealth." *Am. St. Ass'n.,* vol. 11, p. 27. 1908.
Watkins, G. P., and Persons, W. M., " Measurement of Concentration
    of Wealth." *Q. J. Ec.,* vol. 23, p. 160. 1909.
Wright, C. D., " Are the Rich Growing Richer and the Poor, Poorer?"
    Atlantic, vol. 80, p. 300. 1897.
" Amount and Distribution of Incomes," report of a committee of the
    Royal Statistical Society. *J. R. S. S.,* vol. 74, p. 37. 1910.